AUTOMATION AND WORLD COMPETITION

Also by David Wheeler

HUMAN RESOURCE POLICIES, ECONOMIC GROWTH AND
DEMOGRAPHIC CHANGE IN DEVELOPING COUNTRIES

Automation and World Competition

New Technologies, Industrial Location and Trade

Ashoka Mody
Industrial Economist
The World Bank, Washington, D.C.
and
David Wheeler
Associate Professor of Economics
Boston University

St. Martin's Press   New York

First published in the United States of America in 1990

Printed in Singapore

ISBN 0–312–04071–7

Library of Congress Cataloging-in-Publication Data
Mody, Ashoka,
Automation and world competition: new technologies, industrial location
and trade/Ashoka Mody, David Wheeler.
p. cm.
Includes bibliographical references.
ISBN 0–312–04071–7
1. Automation–Economic aspects–Case studies. 2. Textile
industry–Case studies. 3. Clothing trade–Case studies.
4. Electronic industries–Case studies. 5. Automobile industry and
trade–Case studies. 6. Competition, International–Case studies.
I. Wheeler, David, 1946–   II. Title.
HC79.A9M64 1990
338.4'54–dc20   89–28770
                                                                          CIP

To Jyothsna and Trinka

Contents

List of Figures and Tables

FIGURES

TABLES

Acknowledgments

This book would simply not have been possible without a substantial degree of international cooperation. Our work was originally sponsored by the Korean Traders Association and the Korea Development Institute. We are very grateful for their exemplary support and hospitality. We are particularly indebted to Dr Suh Sang-Mok and to Dr Jungho Yoo. In assembling our evidence, we traveled many thousands of miles and interviewed scores of industry specialists in the USA and Asia. For his generous assistance in Japan, we would like to give particular thanks to Dr Saburo Okita. Many thanks also to Dr Shigeru Ishikawa, to Mr Kyoichi Itoh of Toyobo, Ltd., and the production engineering staffs of Toyota and Nissan. In the United States, we owe very considerable debts to Mr Richard Cotton of Dupont Corporation, Mr Howard Dicken of DM Data, and Mr Alfred Bosley of Chrysler Corporation. Many thanks also to our colleagues Gustav Papanek and Leroy Jones for their advice and support.

ASHOKA MODY
DAVID WHEELER

1 Competitive Advantage in the Information Age

Present-day robots can work tirelessly, and they are rapidly growing cheaper. For relatively simple tasks, they are already facile enough to be competitive with high-cost workers in the OECD countries. Their impact on the industrial process is strikingly conveyed by a European textile executive's description of a night visit to an automated textile mill in Japan:

> It is pitch dark... Robots have no eyes, so they need no light. Malfunctions are signalled to a control centre. The problem spot is then lit and a qualified engineer fixes the snag... No more than ten people, boss included, are needed per shift to run the 30,000 ring spindles that represent $22 million in investment.

In the textile sector, at least, it is already possible to displace spindle workers almost completely – at a considerable cost. The analysis of such capabilities and their associated costs is one important theme of this book. Our central purpose is an examination of the competitive dynamics which are emerging in the information age. The three proximate sources of these dynamics are new technologies (such as microelectronics); the search by international firms for low wage sites of production; and the independent emergence of several large low wage countries (such as China, India, Bangladesh and Indonesia) through the development of indigenous management, technological and marketing skills. We investigate the possible impact of these forces on the international distribution of income by studying three industries: garments, semiconductors, and automobiles.

In our empirical analysis, we consider the options and prospects of countries in the high, middle and low-income strata. These will most often be represented by the United States, South Korea and China respectively. Obviously, there is considerable variance in cost and other conditions within the countries of each group. Hence, for

1

example, we include a careful consideration of Japan when examining semiconductors and the Caribbean countries when studying garments. We also make a distinction between middle-income countries and newly industrializing countries (NICs). The latter have attained a certain degree of industrial literacy. Korea and Taiwan are middle-income NICs, but there are also low-wage NICs such as China and India. At present such countries as Indonesia, Philippines, Malaysia and Thailand are moving towards NIC status. They retain the advantage of cheap labor while possessing substantial domestic management and technical capability, but are still constrained by inadequate infrastructure development. In view of their current infrastructure and skills constraints, however, they are not yet prepared to mount an industrial challenge of the Korean type except, perhaps, for strategically-chosen sectors.

Among the three major strands which must be woven together in this book the first is, undeniably, the revolutionary power of electronic microcircuits. The evolution of microelectronics-based technologies has been partly exogenous and partly a response to market forces. The exogeneity has arisen from independent basic research in universities and research laboratories and from the existence of potential physical sources of progress. The best example of physical technical opportunity is the semiconductor, which has witnessed incredible miniaturization in the past two decades; moreover, there is promise of much more before the limits are reached.

Our interest in this book is not on exogenous elements but rather on the incentives to adopt microelectronics technology. In our view, the major incentive has been international competition. World trade grew very rapidly in the two and half decades after the Second World War. The interdependence among nations increased and major new players appeared in international markets. The most viable of these have been Far Eastern countries, particularly Japan, South Korea and Taiwan; Latin American countries, such as Brazil, Mexico and Argentina, have performed erratically, doing very well in some periods and poorly in others. The impact of these new players began to be felt seriously only in the 1970s, when a series of international economic ills slowed the expansion of world trade. The existence of more players, competing for a slower growing pie, has led to two related trends in industrialized economies: increased emphasis on cost reduction at the firm level and the gradual erection of national trade barriers, reversing the trade liberalization trend on the 1950s and 1960s.

To the extent that the new technologies are successful in raising productivity, there will be more for everyone. However, the technologies will not be available to all either because they are covered by intellectual property protection or because they are not easy to learn. Our focus will be on the learning problem. Firms all over the world will face difficult choices: While older technologies threaten to become obsolete, the new ones offer highly uncertain returns. Commitment to using them will be irreversible in some ways: along with "learning-by-doing" with one technology comes "forgetting by not doing" with another. An important task for this book is to document the input requirements of current and expected technologies and to provide quantitative measures of the factors that will influence the location of production in the next round of world competition.

A number of studies of aggregate productivity change have concluded that productivity growth slowed down considerably after the early 1970s. Bailey (1985) has studied US productivity at a sectoral level and finds evidence of deceleration. Taken along with evidence of decline in R&D to sales ratios, some have argued that the stock of technical possibilities has been partially depleted (Evenson, 1984; Scherer, 1978; 1984). On the other hand, the popular impression is one of great ferment in microelectronics, biotechnology and the new materials technologies. Microelectronics, in particular, has entered production processes in many industrial sectors; it is also changing the way many services are produced and distributed. The aggregative statistical evidence on productivity change therefore needs to be interpreted with caution.[1]

It is possible, although unlikely, that microelectronics does not have the potential to foster significant productivity gains. It is quite likely that this new technology is still being used inefficiently by many firms. It is certainly true that the new technologies often require large capital investments and that exploiting their potential requires substantial learning investments. Most firms, even in advanced industrialized nations, are only beginning the process of coming down the learning curve for highly automated flexible manufacturing systems. Investment in learning and differing learning speeds will, therefore, be critical to achieving international competitiveness.

There is also sufficient X-inefficiency in existing production systems for important productivity gains to be realized without the use of new technologies. As part of the general drive towards cost reduction, for example, increased emphasis is being placed on production management to rationalize work flows and inventories. Such improvement essentially entails better information generation and utilization. In the past, microelectronics has not been essential to this process; the Japanese methods of work organization and just-in-time inventory pre-date the introduction of microelectronics on the factory floor. However, there is considerable evidence that future productivity improvements in this area will be related to better use of computing and communication facilities.

Our study suggests that productivity is indeed advanced by the appropriate use of microelectronics technology. Productivity should be understood in a multidimensional sense here. While the saving of human labor is an obvious competitive advantage of the new technology, its contributions to product quality, market response time, and production flexibility are probably more valuable in a number of industries. Indeed, many Western firms have focused on precisely these latter contributions as the key to new product differentiation strategies which (they hope) will sustain profitability even as their competitive position in standard product lines is eroded by their rapidly-advancing competitors from Japan and the NICs. Moreover, the impact of microelectronics varies by sector, by product within sector, and more importantly by processes underlying particular products. Such variations have strong implications for the future location of production sites.

The splitting of production processes has important operational implications. First, when different stages of production are located in different countries, integration becomes more difficult and expensive. Firms with experience in such integration have a considerable competitive advantage. Evolving communications technology is undoubtedly reducing the cost, but good measures are unavailable at present. Second, and perhaps more important, there is a dynamic element. Associated with each stage of production is a particular kind of learning. When the stages are geographically dispersed, the learning will be similarly dispersed. This fact conditions the future technology transitions at particular locations.

An interesting example is provided by semiconductor assembly. This has been a labor intensive process carried out in countries with relatively low wages. Recent developments, however, have made possible a significant degree of automation. This has created the incentive to move the assembly process back to the US. However, the American employees of many firms have "forgotten by not doing" semiconductor assembly. Reintroduction has required importing plant supervisors and workers from the lower-wage countries to ease the transition. While a major technological change has occurred, a number of elements from the more labor intensive process have been carried forward. This has made it worthwhile to transfer learning from the "South" to the "North". If US immigration rules had not permitted temporary employee transfers relocation, the reintroduction might never have occurred.

Splitting the production process into component stages has a further advantage. It enables the incorporation of an additional element in cost reduction strategies. Many firms now routinely attempt to source materials and labor inputs on an international basis in order to minimize costs. "Offshore" plant location is an example. Until recently, a marked propensity to move offshore differentiated Western firms from their Japanese counterparts. The latter have relied more on better information flows and manufacturing automation. After the Yen shock of 1985–86, however, Japanese firms seem to have lost confidence in their ability to compete using high-level automation and organization alone. There is increasing evidence that many are poised to join the search for offshore sites.

While Western firms have been looking over their shoulders at the Japanese, and the latter have begun glancing backward at the East Asian NICs, all current signs point to an imminent broadening of the game. It is a staggering fact that as many people will enter the world's labor force during the coming few decades as are currently alive. Most of them will live in Asia, and most of the Asians will live in China or India. Both countries, along with Indonesia, Bangladesh, and other populous states, are now showing serious interest in export-oriented industrial expansion.

In the face of this heightened low-wage competition, the major dilemma for the middle-income countries will be posed by the fact that they may have neither cheap robots nor cheap workers. In front, they face a continuing technological and political challenge. Firms in the advanced countries have responded to the competitive challenge of cheap imports by upgrading their technologies. The cheaper availability of microelectronic circuits is causing a continuing revolution in the methods of product design, manufacturing and distribution. The move to such technologies is reducing the importance of cheap labor; increasing the feasibility of product customization; and permitting quick response to changes in customer demand. At the same time, the governments of the advanced countries are increasing their support for domestic firms, particularly through market restriction policies.

From the rear, the middle-income countries are being threatened by low-wage countries. These countries are attempting to increase their exports on the basis of their cheap labor, using relatively labor-intensive technologies. China, in particular, has sought to increase its level of international trade. An important feature of this process is the rapprochement between China and the United States, which has led to an opening of the US market to a wide variety of labor-intensive Chinese products. India, Bangladesh, Indonesia and other countries could also play significant roles in the future.

In this flux, the middle income NICs are making large investments in technology. Some, like Korea and Taiwan, are exploring the frontiers of modern technological capabilities to identify their niches. Our analysis shows that such efforts will have to be undertaken even by low wage countries, though not necessarily to the same degree. As we see, semi-automated techniques in some sectors and processes now dominate manual techniques.

SOURCES OF COMPETITIVE ADVANTAGE

Underlying the development of microelectronics, the impetus to source and locate globally and the entry of low wage, skilled and unskilled labor are more fundamental considerations. On the supply side, world competitive advantage is currently being driven by three factors: (1) technological change; (2) institutional development; and (3) strategic behavior of firms and governments. The latter two considerations have become more important because the pace of technical change has quickened. More rapid technical change requires strong institutional development for the acquisition and absorption of technology; and the growth of international trade (with the ensuing increase in international interdependence) has greatly enhanced the role of strategic responses in determining competitiveness.

Technological Change

Throughout this study, we have been impressed by the importance of human knowledge as the driving force of international economic competition. Knowledge enters the production process at different levels. The product is conceived and designed, it is manufactured and distributed. We have been mainly concerned with manufacturing efficiency, although it cannot always be sharply distinguished from productivity in the other stages.

From the point of view of a firm, there are two ways in which manufacturing efficiency can be improved. One form of such progress, which is under the control of the firm, is characterized as "learning-by-doing". It involves the acquisition of production skills in order to operate more efficiently the existing stock of plant and equipment. The other form is much less under the control of the firm; it involves the availability of improved equipment (alternatively referred to as new vintages or generations of capital goods).

Learning-by-Doing

"Learning" is a form of technical progress that takes place after the product and process have been devised in the R&D lab and the required capital equipment has been installed. Learning requires the *use* of the machines. Every new generation of capital goods brings new features which have to be understood by production workers before the full efficiency of the machines can be realized.

Learning takes several different forms. It includes: "improvement in plant layout, changes in the tolerances to which parts are machined, vocational training of the work force, improved communication, and better methods of management" (Sahal, 1981, p. 306). These different facets of learning are of varying importance across industries.

In semiconductor production, learning involves improvements in process control and is measured by greater yields (or larger numbers of integrated circuits per silicon wafer). Unfortunately for would-be entrants, learning is not a deterministic process. Improvement in yields is often the result of improvisation (or "tricks") rather than of strict scientific procedure. There is also a systematic component to learning. In any case, both the systematic and random facets of learning are speeded up by the presence of experienced engineers and technicians.

In the auto industry, learning takes place at two levels. When a new product is introduced, a period of about one year is needed to "fine tune" the manufacturing process. The auto industry is sufficiently complex, however, that it is more profoundly affected by long-term organizational learning about the coordination of industrial processes. We discuss this dimension extensively in Chapter 4. Here we will simply note that superior organizational learning has been the key to the recent development of strong competitive advantage by the Japanese auto industry. Facets of this learning include the "job enlargement" approach, whereby workers are trained to be multi-skilled rather than monoskilled, as in the US industry. The possession of a number of skills improves work flows and eventually reduces costs.

In the textile/garment industries, learning has generally been equated with worker training over a few weeks. While this has traditionally been true in spinning, weaving, and sewing, some operations prior to sewing in garment production have involved skills which require years to develop fully. These included "grading, marking and cutting" – the alteration of basic garment patterns for different body sizes; laying out the patterns so as to minimise fabric wastage; and cutting multiple fabric layers into pieces simultaneously. However, with the introduction of computer controlled systems, these forms of individual learning are rapidly becoming obsolescent. As in semiconductor and automobile production, organizational or "systems" learning is becoming even more important.

There are three dimensions of the learning process which have important implications for competitive advantage but which have received inadequate theoretical and empirical attention:

1. Learning involves an explicit use of resources. An important example is provided by engineers on the shop floor, who are specifically assigned to the task of devising methods for reducing manufacturing costs. In the recent economics and business literature, it has become conventional to assume that learning is a function of cumulative output. This assumption implies that there is no explicit use of resources during the process of learning. However, the engineers in all our target industries have insisted that learning can be speeded up by employing resources devoted to the task.

2. Learning about a particular technology always takes place with the knowledge that a new technology of production (embodied in superior capital goods) will arrive at some time in the future and render the learning on the old technology largely irrelevant. Such uncertainty has a significant impact on the optimal time stream of resources devoted to learning.

3. If learning is human resource intensive, then another issue of importance arises. After the engineers have performed the

learning function (and hence reduced costs), can they be dispensed with? The answer depends very much on whether the knowledge embodied in the engineers is transferable to production workers. If the knowledge cannot be codified into rule books, then the removal of an engineer will lead to "forgetting" and a bumping up of production costs.

These considerations suggest that the extent of learning that will be undertaken by a private firm will depend upon the wage rates of specialized manufacturing engineers (who perform the learning); the discount rate and time horizon of the firm; the uncertainty of the firm about the arrival of the new technology (embodied in new capital equipment); and the difference in skills between manufacturing engineers and production workers (who have to carry on the task once the specialized engineers leave).

Policy Implications of Learning

One theme of recent trade and industrial policy discussions in the United States has been the need to protect domestic industry, thus allowing it time to "come down the learning curve" and become internationally competitive. A similar theme has had an important influence on the theory and practice of development economics. In the case of developing countries, we now have about three decades of experience which shows that learning is sometimes achieved and sometimes not. Protection of the domestic market appears to be necessary for achieving cost reduction through learning in at least some industries, but there is nothing automatic or god-given about learning even when the firm is positioned in a protected market. Since protection imposes definite costs, the indefinite continuation of protection is unlikely to be good policy. On the other hand, if the policy is to gradually phase out the protection, the extent of learning undertaken may be reduced in anticipation of the phasing out. The results of short-run intervention via trade policy could go either way. In the long run, it is a country's institutional development and human resource policies which will be critical.

Product Cycles

There is much empirical evidence which suggests that product cycles are shorter than they used to be. The length of the product cycle has essentially been driven by the availability of new forms of capital equipment. One has to be somewhat careful here in defining a *product.* Strictly speaking, new generations of superior capital equipment improve the price/performance ratio of a generic product; the improvements are marketed as new products that are close substitutes for the previous product generation. On account of the superior price/performance ratio, the new supercedes the old. The most dramatic example of such supercession comes from the market for semiconductor memories. Succeeding generations of memories have packed greater memory capacity onto the same silicon area. This has been made possible by the evolution of production equipment that could define ever smaller memory cells. Similar improvements in price/performance ratios have occured in industries as diverse as textiles and automobiles.

What is the force behind the rapid improvement of capital goods? Is there some commonality which is driving the improvements simultaneously across these diverse sectors? These are complex questions and there clearly are several answers. One facet of great importance, however, is the increasing incorporation of microelectronics. The main economic function of microelectronics is to process vast amounts of information at very rapid rates and at low cost; the improved information availability then makes possible greater control over the production process. Such control increases speed and reduces waste. Automation must be considered but one facet of this generic capability of information processing.

It should be clearly stated, to avoid any misunderstanding, that the trend towards embodiment of microelectronics in capital goods is still young; the "lights-out", fully-automated factory described at the beginning of this chapter is still a rarity. The constraints to full automation include organizational inertia, new knowledge and skill requirements and uncertainty about the productivity gains from automation.[2] It is possible that product cycles are also being shortened by more rapid changes in consumer tastes, but this is an aspect which we have not studied in any depth.

Absolute Dominance

Related to shortening product cycles and improving price/ performance ratios is the idea of absolute dominance. The response of most western economies to the exports of NICs has been to invest in new technology development. Such technologies have been capital and knowledge intensive. More importantly, they have tended to be more efficient than earlier technologies: For a unit of output, they use a smaller *total* input value than more labor intensive processes.

The implication clearly is that the middle income or even the low wage countries cannot in many instances continue to use labor intensive technologies if they are to be internationally competitive. This is not a universal phenomenon, of course. Our research results show, for example, that at Chinese wage rates the most labor intensive technology is still the most competitive in some kinds of textile production. Even in that industry (and more so in the apparel industry) the general trend toward greater capital intensity can be discerned.

There is a further set of factors which reduce the desirability of adopting a labor intensive technology. It has been argued for a long time that a capital intensive technology increases the value-added share of the "capitalist" and hence provides greater reinvestible resources. But a new consideration is emerging – the phenomenon of "technology neighborhoods".

Technology Neighborhoods

In traditional technology systems, the production skills differed considerably across product lines. In the late nineteenth and early twentieth centuries, the flow system of organization began to dominate and at the same time cut across different product types (in continuous flow industries and also in industries which required assembly, where the assembly line provided the basis of the flow principle). The flow principle thus provided a technology neighborhood in the sense that experience with working on a product line could be largely transferred to the production of a completely different product because the underlying technology was similar.

A new neighborhood is now emerging as a consequence of the spread of information technology. Widely different product groups are already sharing (or will share in the near future) common methods of using this new technology.[3] In this respect, continuing with traditional labor intensive methods could prove to be the wrong social decision in the long run. Indeed, it might ensure that sufficient production skills required to operate information-based technologies would simply not be available.

Institutional Development and Human Resources

In the context of the technology trends described above, appropriate institutional development and human resource policies become critical.

Institutions

The evolution of the dynamic comparative advantage of a country can be conceptualized in the following manner. At any given time, individual firms try to anticipate their future comparative advantage and make investment decisions to *realize* that advantage. In other words, an expectation is formed regarding what the appropriate products and technologies will be some years down the line; steps are taken to put in place a production system that would be relevant to those products and technologies. The results generated by the sum of the micro decisions of individual firms add up to the revealed comparative advantage of the country.

These simple considerations point to the importance of two factors relevant for the successful evolution of comparative advantage: (1) the efficiency of information acquisition and assimilation; (2) the timing of commitment (or entry) and the ability to make the necessary investments. Both factors tend to favor the growth of large diversified firms.

Information acquisition and assimilation

This is not a very well understood issue. There are some *a priori* reasons to believe, in the current state of wide information dispersal, that large firms have no differential advantage in this respect. In fact, some are inclined to argue that improved information availability should favor small firms, enhancing their inherent flexibility. Such a view misses two important (and related) issues: (1) the possibility of *misinformation*; and (2) the need to process *facts* (which are widely available) into information (which is not widely available).

Undoubtedly the technology of facts generation has improved greatly, and thus facts are available at low cost. However, there is still a need to choose facts which are relevant. Such choice requires some theoretical understanding of the process for which the facts are being sought. Presumably, such understanding is embodied in "experts". If such expertise requires a fixed cost commitment, as is likely to be the case when experts are employed in-house, then there will be scale economies in the use of expert knowledge. Similarly, the transformation of facts into information is also likely to be characterized by scale economies. For these and other similar reasons, large firms may always have a *differential advantage* in information acquisition and use.[4] It is, of course, possible to buy expert services from various sources;[5] to that extent, scale economies will be less important.

Timing of entry and capital markets

The transition to capital and knowledge intensive technologies depends a great deal on the timing of entry into the market. Early entry is usually desirable. The new technologies require a period of experimentation in order to reduce costs and, more recently, product life-cycles have tended to be short, narrowing the window of opportunity. However, there is some advantage in being a latecomer if significant resources can be deployed towards buying the experience of others and avoiding their mistakes. Also, it is possible to gain an advantage over competitors by installing the most recent generation of capital goods.

In order to take advantage of being a latecomer, it is essential that the appropriate institutional framework be in place. The importance of appropriate institutions is brought out by comparing Korea and Taiwan. These two countries have begun making a successful transition to knowledge and capital intensive industries. Of the two, however, Korea has been significantly more aggressive (the most dramatic demonstration being the recent Korean acquisition of advanced semiconductor production capability, making Korea, after the US and Japan, the world's third most sophisticated producer of semiconductor memories). Over the last two decades, the Korean government has been active in promoting the conglomerate form of firm organization. This organizational mode has served as a substitute for the capital market and is today permitting very large scale investment in high technology ventures.

It should be noted that the emergence of the Korean conglomerates has been encouraged by explicit government policy over the last two decades. In Taiwan, the absence of similar firm organization has led to a different form of government intervention. The Taiwanese government is currently providing entrepreneurs (both domestic and overseas Chinese) a number of incentives to develop the high technology sectors. These incentives include tax breaks and other forms of subsidization. They also include an effort to promote a government backed research and service organization, which is in the nature of a public good and is expected to lower entry barriers for entrepreneurs. To summarize, in both Korea and Taiwan, we see an attempt to overcome market failures. In Korea, the market has been bypassed in favor of large domestic firms; in Taiwan, government intervention for the provision of public goods is still called for.[6]

Human resource policies

Progress in the development of educational infrastructure worldwide will continue to promote rapid development of skills at all levels. This expansion will have two features of primary importance. At advanced levels, it will assure a continuing fall in the price of the engineering and technical skills which are complementary to information capital in its various forms. At more basic levels, the impact of education will interact strongly with another emerging phenomenon: The near-simultaneous movement toward more active world market participation of the current and future population giants of Asia: China, India, Bangladesh, Pakistan, and Indonesia.[7] If it continues, this extroversion will ensure steady outward movement of the world labor supply curve for decades and an effective fall in the price of literate labor. Basic labor is a substitute for capital, so this development produces forces antithetical to those generated by the "high technology revolution".

To keep pace with these forces, newly-industrializing countries have the task of developing further their own educational infrastructures. As we have indicated in the previous section, knowledge for manufacturing capability needs to be acquired and assimilated at many different levels. There is training required at the level of production workers, there is experience needed at the level of organizational supervisors and there is need for a general community which can generate new ideas. This is unfortunately not a task that can be accomplished overnight.

Strategic Considerations

Appropriate institutional development permits the firms of a country to become potential players in the international marketing game. However, that is not sufficient. The game has to be played, and, in general, has to be played against stronger rivals.[8]

For about 30 years in the post Second World War period, international trade grew at a faster pace than world production. This led to the increasing integration of national economies into a world system. One consequence of this integration has been that even in a large economy such as the United States, international competitors are no longer viewed as fringe or minor rivals; rather they are viewed as serious competitors against whom strategic initiatives are required. Similarly, the Japanese producers, after having stormed the world markets for a few decades, are facing the prospect of competition from new players in the international game. They are responding by staking out strategic positions in key markets through a combination of rapid improvement in their technology and aggressive pricing.

Strategic interaction has become important not merely at the level of the firms. Indeed, some would argue that strategic game playing at the level of governments has had a more important impact on world trade. The trend towards increased "protectionism" or "managed trade" or "industrial policy" reflects keener government involvement in international trade. Below, we sketch some general issues relating to strategic interaction both at the firm and government levels.

Firm strategies

The key issue of relevance to newly industrializing countries is: "How can the disadvantages of being late be overcome?" This is no longer merely a question of appropriate technology acquisition, but rather the ability to respond to price and non-price competitive weapons of the "incumbent" firms. There is a long tradition in the international organization literature of examining how *dominant* firms emerge and whether they are likely to *persist*. The emergence of dominance is seen as the consequence of early investment in capacity, product differentiation, and economies of scale. In the words of Geroski and Jacquemin (1984, p. 3), a dominant firm possesses the ability "to precommit itself to a strategic position which narrows the range of replies open to its rival". Such pre-commitment may either be purely fortuitous or due to the early spotting of a new opportunity. Once the options of the rivals have been narrowed by some strategic action, the dominant firm can derive monopoly profits from the system.

The persistence of monopoly profits depends on whether the strategic actions of the firms are subject to depreciation (which includes the possibility that exogenous technical progress may create conditions for a new race). Besides the possibility of exogenous change, there is a view that the dominant firm may indeed be maximizing its net present value by permitting some entry. In order to keep out potential entrants, the dominant firm has to forego short-term profits. Particularly when entry is random, it is optimal to derive the short-term rents from the position of dominance and risk some entry.[9]

It is useful to look at some recent examples. In the 1960s and the early 1970s, US firms enjoyed a position of dominance in a number of industries. In major product lines such as steel, autos, textiles, and electronics, these firms have now ceded their dominance. In contrast, the Japanese firms, which have acquired dominant positions in the last decade in the auto and electronics industries, have until recently made strenuous efforts to hang on to their leadership positions. It should be noted, though, that even Japanese firms have ceded their dominant position in the shipping industry. It is clear that the Japanese encroachment on US dominance has very largely been a function of quick response to windows of opportunity opened up by technical change or other structural shifts. In the auto industry, for example, the oil crisis of the 1970s and the ensuing environmental regulations created a transitional period during which the US industry had to readjust. The Japanese firms were able to take advantage of this transitional period. In the electronics industry, the rapid pace of technical change has continuously generated the possibility of market niches which have allowed initial entry; the Japanese have then built on their manufacturing strengths to forge into mass markets.

However, technical change and structural shifts are not the entire explanation of Japanese entry into markets traditionally held by US firms. It is also true that US firms have enjoyed significant profit margins in industries that have been "targeted" by the Japanese. These high margins could have arisen for two reasons: (1) the US firms were willing to allow the possibility of entry in order to make short-term profits; there may have been a misperception that they were so far ahead that entry by non-US firms was unlikely; (2) any decision to deter entry would have required the combined action of the US firms. This creates the classic public goods problem: Deterrent action by one firm imposes the cost of deterrence mainly on that firm but spreads the benefits to the others.

The issue for the middle-income NICs in the current context is whether recent structural and technical changes, on the one hand, and the investment behavior of the Japanese and US firms, on the other hand, will be such as to allow them entry into new markets. There are two considerations to take into account. First, the NIC firm must be able to take advantage of transitional periods of technical and structural change. This, as was discussed above, requires the development of appropriate institutions. Brazil, for example, attempted to break into the minicomputer and microcomputer markets in periods of technical transition (during which the large multinationals had not developed a strong interest in these markets).[10] However, while the interest was there and the time was right, the Brazilians were unable to develop strong institutions which could take advantage of the opportunity.

Secondly, the Japanese have apparently been more aggressive in their investment behavior (and hence in their deterrence of new entrants) than the US firms were in the earlier period vis-a-vis the Japanese firms. For example, the Japanese have been unwilling to give up their hold over what would normally be regarded as *mature* products. Korean and Taiwanese firms have tried to produce micro-computer floppy disk drives for the world market; however, the Japanese have sought to automate and refine their production systems at a rapid pace and have thus denied significant access to the market. Similarly, the Japanese continue to improve their methods of television production.[11] To summarize, current world conditions are such that the breaking into markets held by a few dominant firms is likely to more difficult than in the 1970s.

Government strategies

In discussing the role of the government in promoting institutional development, we pointed out that such development was a response to the need for correcting market failures. However, the government may, and does, intervene even when there is no explicit market failure. In a world trading system characterized by imperfect competition and hence by strategic firm interaction, the government has an interest in strengthening the strategic hand of its firms.

A simple example would be the subsidization of the exports of a domestic monopolist. In a world of perfect competition, such subsidization would not improve national welfare: the increase in profits to the firm would be offset by the cost of the subsidy to the government. However, in a situation of imperfect competition, the knowledge of the government subsidy increases the aggressiveness of the domestic firm, which then makes a commitment to bolder output and pricing decisions in world markets. The rival firm backs off in view of this threat and allows the subsidized firm to take a larger share of the market. The increase in profits of the domestic firm in this situation is greater than the subsidy and hence there is a gain in national welfare.[12]

There are at least two difficulties with such strategic behavior on the part of governments. First, there will be an incentive for every government to play the strategic game, and depending on the nature of the game, reducing not just total world welfare but also the welfare of their own countries. Secondly, there is nothing to guarantee that firms will respond in an aggressive manner when they are backed by domestic subsidization. There is enough evidence from developing and developed countries to suggest that subsidization may well form the focus of rent seeking. Although there are notable exceptions, many Western firms have complemented their market strategies with a political strategy – agitation for protection from "unfair" competition. Trade barriers are rising rapidly, in forms which violate the spirit of existing trade agreements while preserving the letter. One popular form is the "voluntary" export restraint (VER), which has assumed particular prominence in the automobile and garment industries. The VER allows producers in both the exporting and the importing country to benefit. Total supply is restricted and prices are therefore bid up, with the consumer being worse off, at least in the short run. The attractiveness of the VER lies in its ease of administration and in the appeasement of producer lobbies.

When domestic industries have felt profoundly threatened and "voluntary" restraints have not materialized rapidly enough, "dumping" charges have proven popular as a bludgeon. "Dumping" has proven appealing as a concept because its inherent plasticity makes formal trade agreements easy to circumvent. The oldest and simplest definition of dumping involves comparison of an exporter's prices in domestic and international markets. If the domestic market price is higher, the producer is considered to be "dumping" his output overseas. The reigning assumption in such cases is generally that the producer is implicitly subsidizing exports by charging high prices in the domestic market. US electronics firms have found this definition to be useful in a number of actions against Japanese and other Far Eastern competitors.

More recently, these competitors have proven sufficiently formidable that "dumping" has had to assume a new incarnation. During the recent past, the major Japanese semiconductor firms have been accused (and found "guilty") of dumping semiconductor memories in the United States. In this case, however, there is no evidence of discriminatory pricing (in fact, prices in Japan may well have been lower than those in the US). In a conceptual leap which has gladdened the hearts of US semiconductor producers, the US Commerce Department has decided that "dumping" will henceforth be defined as pricing below "fair market value". This value, in turn, is to be determined by analysis of the actual production costs of Japanese firms. This field is obviously wide open for creative political accounting.[13]

SECTORAL ANALYSES

The purpose of this study is to examine the recent determinants of competitive advantage in three very different industries: semiconductors, automobiles and textiles/garments. We have chosen to study three quite distinct sectors rather than attempt a more ambitious intersectoral analysis. In a recent study of the impact of automation on employment, Leontief and Duchin (1986) considered the entire economy, which they divided into 89 sectors. They were thus able to study intersectoral linkages and hence account for the direct effects within sectors and the indirect effects of automation in those sectors on the economy as a whole. There are conceptual as well as empirical reasons for our more selective approach. Conceptually, we are interested in studying the impact of productivity change; Leontief and Duchin were primarily interested in the increasing capital-intensity of production. We thus need to explicitly consider the costs of producing a product with alternative technologies: such costs determine the choice of technology. In order to understand technology choice, we have had to study more closely the institutional and strategic environment of the particular sector and also study the quantitative dimensions of the sub-processes within each sector. Such an effort for the entire economy was clearly out of our reach.

The three industries we have chosen span the current technological spectrum. The semiconductor industry has for long been a symbol of "high-tech"; the auto industry has been characterized by a much slower pace of innovation but is nevertheless a technologically and organizationally complex industry; the textile/garment sectors have retained a labor-intensive character, though as we shall discuss below, there are signs of significant technical change even within this group of industries. The results of the empirical analysis show that some stages of garment production may now be cost effectively produced in the industrialized countries using automated techniques; on the other hand, the NICs that can learn at a rapid rate and those that have an adequate infrastructure may well be in a position to efficiently produce advanced semiconductor devices. In other words, the nature of technological progress is changing the characteristics of industries and that requires a change in the way we think about them. In Table 1.1, we list other features which differentiate the three industries.

TABLE   1.1 *Distinguishing   industry   characteristics: semiconductors,*
                 automobiles and textiles/garments

Industry characteristic	Semiconductors	Automobiles	Textiles/garments
Structure of industry	Competitive/ oligopolistic	Oligopolistic	Competitive
	Medium to large-sized firms	Large firms	Few large and many small firms
Barriers to entry	Medium and increasing because of high capital costs	High but decreasing because of cheaper distribution costs	Low and increasing because of high capital costs
Degree of vertical integration	Low	High	Generally low, but high for a few
Product differentiability	Traditionally very little, but increasing in importance	High, but may decrease	Varies greatly
Length of product cycle	4–8 years	4–10 years	Several weeks to many years
Sources of growth	Process innovations and new capital goods	Reducing existing X-inefficiency and new capital goods	Improved technology embodied in new capital goods
Technology flow	Internal R&D, cross-licencing	Mainly internal efforts	Mainly external sources
Length of learning period	2–3 years	1 year for a single model; 6–8 years for more general learning	2 weeks–3 years for traditional technologies; 1–2 years for automation

   The differences in the three industries arise partly because of their
different physical characteristics and partly because of their different
historical evolution. Some of these issues are discussed in the
individual industry chapters. Here we wish to stress the common

features and major themes that emerge from the cross-industry comparison.

We begin the book with an analysis of the emerging competitive dynamics in garments and textiles. These are industries in which NICs like Korea and Hong Kong have built and maintained major export positions based on low-wage labor. Recent developments in these two sectors reflect all the major determinants of competitive advantage which we described previously. On the one hand, both textiles and garments have the potential for near-total automation. The requisite technologies are unquestionably in place, or soon will be. At the same time, however, China, Bangladesh, Indonesia, and other large, poor states are entering the international game in force. China has shown particular competitive vigor. As a result, firms in both NICs and the OECD countries are faced with critical strategic choices. In the coming competition, which products and/or processes can be captured by automated systems? Where are such systems likely to be located? Which products/processes will retain sufficient labor intensity to contribute to export expansion by the new low-wage exporters?

We continue our analysis with a discussion of semiconductor memories – a high-technology industry in which the US and Japan are totally dominant but potentially threatened by a number of aspirants among the OECD countries and NICs. Semiconductor production has been described by trade economists as "classically nonclassical" – product cycles are extremely short; capital costs are huge and unavoidable; the productivity differential associated with superior engineering techniques is enormous; and movement down the learning curve is critically affected by the existing technological support base. In this arena, the success of potential NIC entrants like Korea is far from certain. If they can match US and Japanese learning speeds, their lower personnel costs would give them a competitive advantage. But will their limited technological base allow them to move down the learning curve fast enough to justify the enormous automation which must be undertaken? With the advent of advanced automation and even steeper learning curves in the US and Japan, is the commitment to advanced semiconductors too risky at this stage for NICs to undertake?

Finally, we consider competitive dynamics in compact automobile production. Since the aspirations of most exporters are clearly focused on North America at this stage, we will focus on competitive dynamics at the entry level in the North American market.

In the entry-level auto market, emergent firms in countries like Korea, Malaysia, Yugoslavia, and Brazil have several problems to consider. Among them is the potential for a competitive response through automation by both US and Japanese firms. Strategic behavior by firms and governments will also play a central role, as will the evolution of consumer demand if fuel prices stabilize at low levels for a number of years. Finally, there is the emerging threat of a small vehicle glut as Japanese producers ramp up in the US and the new aspirants begin moving large numbers of small vehicles to market.

SIMULATING COST DYNAMICS

As the centerpiece of the three sectoral analyses, we will present the results of our quantitative modeling exercises. The computer model which we have employed is described below. As economists we have found that the design of an appropriate model has required the recognition of certain hard truths. First, we have had to abandon conventional econometric approaches. Since robotic factories scarcely exist, there is no established database and econometric estimation of production functions is simply impossible. Secondly, we have had to drop our economist's comfortable assumption that broad product classes are meaningful aggregates. To find out about automation, one has to speak to the engineers – the people who are bringing it into being. Engineers, to their credit, do not make generalizations which they know to be inappropriate. They will not admit to knowing much about producing "garments", for example, but they can talk all day long about producing men's long-sleeve cotton dress shirts or women's high style printed polyester dresses. For it turns out that particular garments are produced by processes so different that they can be regarded as economically "similar" only to their ultimate consumers.

Engineers are also uncomfortable with the notion of "smooth substitution possibilities" between labor and capital. In their world production proceeds in stages, each of which can be performed with a variety of possible technologies. At each stage, the process of production itself is performed at stations where human workers and machines share out the tasks in different measure. Some workers are also employed in the transfer of materials between stations, and others busy themselves with maintenance and cleaning.

In this world of specific processes and products, smooth substitution possibilities are not common. At each process stage, the need for industry standardization leads to the clustering of technologies around capital/labor ratios which are roughly appropriate to differing economic circumstances. Once a basic process technology is chosen, the substitution process narrows to choices about the degree of mechanization of transfers between stations, cleaning work, etc.

As economists, we have derived great intellectual profit from this exposure to the world of the engineers. It is cluttered, but undeniably compelling. And in any case, to analyze automation possibilities we have had to play the game on their court. We have therefore constructed models for our target industries which are tightly focused on products, stages of production, and technologies. While laying the foundation for such models was extraordinarily time-consuming, we have found that the engineering approach yields a number of compensating benefits.

First, when production is modeled as a series of processes, it is possible to replicate the true international division of labor in many product lines. At the present time, for example, it is quite common for garments to be designed in one country, the fabric marked and cut in a second, sewn in a third, and sold in a fourth. Secondly, the division of production into stages allows for explicit consideration of the fact that internal rates of technological progress can differ. Fabrics are now routinely patterned, marked, and cut by automated systems, but sewing has remained a hard, expensive automation problem and labor-intensive sewing still dominates. Until recently, the same asymmetry between pre-assembly and assembly activities characterized semiconductor memory production. In automobile assembly plants, painting and welding are now routinely done by robots but intricate component installation tasks require extremely expensive machines. By breaking our treatment of production down into process stages, we have been able to model this kind of asymmetry.

Finally, of course, our focus on engineering specifications has allowed us to bring the best available engineering knowledge and experience to bear on the central question of our project: During the next decade, what automation possibilities will exist, how much labor can be replaced, and at what cost?

After a period of intensive work, we have arrived at a modeling approach which, as far as we know, is not available elsewhere. For each product which we consider, we have detailed process specifications broken down by stage of production. At each stage, we allow for a variety of existing technologies, and for the next phase of robotic technology. In each case, all major input requirements and costs are specified. For consideration of the full competitive implications of the alternative technologies and costs, we have written a computer model which has substantial power and flexibility. It is explicitly dynamic in that it allows for the inclusion of engineering estimates of process-specific learning speeds. It also accounts for the extra resources which are required for learning to be accelerated.

Our model has an explicit locational component. It allows production to be broken up by stages, and considers the relative economic efficiency of all technologies (including soon-to-arrive robotic technology) for each stage at alternative possible production sites. Transport costs and differential tariff charges are calculated. Finally, the model keeps time accounts as well as cost accounts. It keeps track of time in production, time in transit between process stages, and time spent in inventory storage. We view this time-accounting feature as important because the capacity for rapid production response is growing in importance as a source of competitive advantage. One of the advantages of advanced technologies is that they are often much faster than their labor-intensive counterparts.

In each sectoral analysis, we use the capabilities of the model which seem most appropriate to the circumstances. In garments, for example, we give strong emphasis to location-specific costs by production stage. In textiles and semiconductors, we consider costs associated with multi-stage production undertaken with alternative technologies and costs for integrated final assembly plants. In all cases we allow for differential learning speeds, although these are much more important for some products and technologies than for others.

2 The Garment and Textile Industries

Two major forces are promoting dramatic change in the prospective international division of labor in garments and textiles.[1] Producers in the NICs are now looking over their shoulders at nascent garment and textile export operations in the newly-invigorated economies of the Asian population giants – China, India, Indonesia, Bangladesh, and Pakistan. Concurrently with this increase in wage-based competition, sophisticated microelectronics-based systems for garment and textile production and marketing are emerging in the OECD economies.

Rather suddenly, then, the NICs face the prospect of an unprecedented squeeze. Their garment/textile industries show signs of drifting simultaneously toward "sunset", in the direction of the new low-wage competitors, and towards "sunrise" in the West. In the industrial economies these industries are reverting to infant industry status. Our analysis suggests that an overwhelming drift toward sunset would materialize in the absence of state intervention in the pattern of international trade. With the continuation of current trade management practices, however, it is possible to foresee quite a different outcome. In order to reinforce this point, we will begin our treatment of the topic with a "Western" scenario.

Robotics, in this scenario, is identified as a critical infant industry in the West. Behind protective barriers, OECD manufacturers have the time and investible surplus necessary to consolidate and restructure their operations for automated production. Guaranteed a relatively large market, the producers of automated systems come down their own learning curves and deliver products at ever-decreasing costs, adjusted for quality. Finally, producers in the low-wage economies find that they cannot even maintain their formerly quota-constrained market shares. Their first response (as is currently the case for the NICs) is to find products whose small batch sizes and complex stitching requirements render automation relatively costly. This competitive margin shrinks inexorably, however, as robotic technology gets more powerful. By the year 2000, the robots reign supreme in the world garment and textile markets.

Just how likely are we to move to the final act of this scenario in the next decade? We are currently only at curtain rise, as some firms in the OECD countries have begun responding to competition by investing in the new microelectronics based technology. Undeniably, this is providing substantial possibilities for cost reduction, particularly in the pre-assembly phase; it also permits significant reductions in process time and faster response to demand changes. In addition, the appeal of quick market response has stimulated a growing tendency to restrict offshore locations to nearby areas. The rate of new technology adoption is still relatively slow because the industry (in particular, the garment sector) has traditionally consisted of very small firms. There is, however, increasing evidence of consolidation as progressive firms move to a scale appropriate for automated manufacturing.

In important recent work, Hoffman and Rush (1985; 1988) have concluded that the Western technologists' vision is correct – microelectronics technology will have an overwhelming influence on garment manufacturing. They document, on the basis of extensive field work, the productivity gains which are now possible for large-scale firms in the OECD countries. After analyzing the capabilities and costs of the new technologies, we agree with Hoffman and Rush that their adoption would substantially improve the prospects of these firms in their now-traditional competition with firms in Korea and other NICs such as Taiwan and Hong Kong. However, our analysis also points to the significance of the second major force which we cited above: Large-scale market entry by the low-wage population giants of Asia.

Since producers in the US have traditionally been willing to locate labor-intensive operations in low-wage countries, these new entrants are not entirely unwelcome. China is feared by many (and rightly so, as our modeling exercise will demonstrate), but low-wage sites in the Caribbean, Mexico, and Central America are available to support domestic strategies focused on pre-assembly automation and quick response to market demand. For NICs such as Taiwan and Korea, however, this new development implies a change in competitive status. Until recently, producers of textiles and garments in these countries had few peers in the use of labor-intensive technologies. They could therefore concentrate on integrated, locally-based export operations as part of national drives to acquire the individual and organizational skills necessary for rapid development. In this chapter we shall describe how that is likely to change.

THE CHALLENGE: ASIAN EXPORTS

In garments, we see the genesis of the East Asian challenge. Production by newcomers was normally in basic garments, with entry into more quality- and time-sensitive markets after an intensive period of learning by workers, managers, and organizations. By the late 1970s, Asian production of basic apparel lines was so cost-effective that Western companies faced complete extinction. Only the advent of the microprocessor has given them any hope of stabilizing or recapturing their market share. We will begin the story, then, with a look at the magnitude of the challenge which has been mounted by low-wage production in Asia.

Major International Markets

During the past two decades, expansion into the US market has served as a primary foreign exchange earner for developing states in Asia. In almost every category of apparel, the ratio of imports to total US production has increased significantly from the mid-1960s, and particularly rapidly since the mid-1970s.[2] The four major exporters to the US are Hong Kong, Taiwan, Korea and China. Of these, China is the most recent entrant to the international market. While garments provided a good export platform for the first-generation NICs, the data suggest that the environment will not be as supportive for their aspiring successors. World trade in garments was relatively stable in the early 1980s, decreasing from $39.29 billion in 1980 to $38.47 billion in 1983. Since the price of traded garments has not changed very much, the volume of trade has also remained stable. However, a significant change has taken place in the *direction* of the international garment trade. Together, Europe and the US have accounted for between 80 and 85 per cent of imports in the recent past. However, while US imports have risen significantly, European imports have declined, particularly since 1980. As we will document below, protectionist sentiments are also building rapidly in the US. There are, therefore, only three potential sources of significant growth in world garments and textiles for LDCs during the coming decade.

First, the impact of the "Yen shock" is obviously interfering, at least in the short run, with Japanese plans to renew the competitiveness of their basic manufacturing activities with automated systems. The relative price of low- and medium-technology Japanese manufactured goods have skyrocketed since 1985, and a steady erosion of market share in favor of the NICs has begun. There is now the real possibility that the Japanese will diverge from their traditional development path, choosing instead to follow the path already worn smooth by the US and Western Europe. The new strategy might include more reliance on domestic sources of growth; rapid movement towards services and high technology exports as the mainstays of the economy; and drastically increased dependence on non-Japanese sources of low-and medium-technology manufactured goods. If the Japanese choose this path, there is a very good chance that world trade in garments and textiles can grow significantly even if imports into the US and Western Europe are stable or modestly declining.

Secondly, there is at least some possibility that the COMECON economies will become much more integrated into the world economy during the next decade. Their current technology base and wage levels are such that these economies seem unlikely to adopt either labor-intensive or robotic technologies for garment and textile production. There is a chance, therefore, that the COMECOM economies will become a significant and growing market for LDC exports in these sectors.

Finally, there is the real possiblity of a redistribution of the existing trade shares in garments and textiles. As we will note later in this chapter, much of the current pattern of garment trade is preordained by bilateral agreements governing the allocation of quotas for export to the United States. It is clear that relaxation of these quotas in favor of more general competitive access to the US market would generate sizable increases in market share for low-wage competitors such as China, Philippines, Indonesia and Bangladesh. For the poorest states in Asia, however, even the abolition of quotas would not be without risk. Among the low-wage states, the most efficient producers would stand to gain the most. A comparison of the recent experience of China and Philippines is instructive in this regard.

Relative Success of Newcomers: China and Philippines

China is obviously joining the East Asian NICs as a major player in world apparel and textile markets. Much of China's current competitive advantage in garments comes from its ability to produce cheap fabrics. Our research indicates that the spinning, preparation and weaving stages of fabric production are still more amenable to labor-intensive techniques than the three stages of garment production. Of all the Far Eastern countries, China is able to produce the cheapest fabric. Our model results for textile production (discussed in detail in Appendix 2) suggest that the advent of Robotic textile technology will have only a marginal impact on the current competitive balance. The cost disadvantage of US producers will not be as great as it is now, but it will still be very substantial. The results also suggest that Korean textile producers will be at a substantial cost disadvantage relative to the Chinese.

While China seems to have mastered basic production skills in a relatively brief interval of time, Philippines has not built on its early lead as an East Asian supplier in this industry. Generally, the direction of Philippine exports has followed world trends in the past few years.[3] The share going to the US has increased substantially and that going to Europe has correspondingly declined. But of major concern to Philippines is the fact that it has actually *lost* world market share during this period. Between 1981 and 1983, the loss of share took place in both the US market and in the European market. Since then the loss of share has continued in the European market. The share loss has been largely to "newcomers" such as China, Thailand and Indonesia.

With the recent rapid growth of Japan as an industrial power, it would seem logical to suppose that comparative advantage would have been served by a Philippine shift toward Japan as an alternative market. Indeed, the Japanese market is of considerable interest to countries such as Philippines because it is not explicitly protectionist. Unfortunately, Japanese imports of garments are only a small fraction of world import demand (Japanese demand has been at or below $2 billion, constituting less than 6 per cent of world demand). The lack of growth of the Japanese market does not augur well for countries such as Philippines. Moreover, it should be noted that Philippines has been losing even its small market share in Japan. One country that has expanded its exports to Japan substantially during this period is China.

Why has China performed so well in comparison with Philippines? Philippine wage rates are somewhat higher than Chinese wage rates, but they are still very low. The higher Philippine wage rate, when compared with China, is partially compensated for by somewhat higher productivity. Part of the reason for Philippine difficulties in expanding garment exports undoubtedly lies in the nature of the bargaining which determines international quota allocation. Every nation recognizes the present and potential power of China, and this gives the Chinese tremendous leverage in negotiations. It must be acknowledged, however, that this structural factor scarcely explains the loss of share by Philippine producers in every major market.

A major reason why China has fared so well is the international competitiveness of its domestic fabric-producing sector. As speed of response becomes an increasing necessity for participating in international garment markets, backward linkage into a strong textile sector is rising steadily in importance. Undoubtedly, the deep involvement of Hong Kong textile and apparel firms at all stages of the process in China provides one major key to explaining the recent Chinese success.

Unfortunately, there has been no "Hong Kong factor" in Philippines. Philippine garment production has been dominated by American garment houses. For the most part, these firms have produced non-seasonal, low fashion apparel such as children's wear and undergarments. They have shown little inclination to promote the kind of worker and organizational learning which would lead to enhanced competitiveness. Japanese investors do not seem to have done better. The usual explanations given by the Japanese trading companies for lack of interest in buying from Philippines for the Japanese market are:

1. Philippines lack special materials to produce high quality garments. In theory, such materials could be imported, but high value goods also require quicker response time.
2. Philippine design sense and sewing techniques are immature.
3. Philippine delivery times are poor.

Despite these complaints, Japanese joint venture companies have typically not trained the Philippine workforce to improve sewing techniques or design sense. Indeed, the joint ventures do not perform any better than the average Philippine firm in their ability to export to Japan.

The joint ventures apparently have failed to promote the two kinds of learning which seem essential for enhanced competitiveness in garments. Most industry specialists agree that large production runs of a particular garment are essential to come down the learning curve and make a profit on the production of that garment; learning occurs on each variation of the garment, so, for example, it is not enough to produce several blouses, but rather long runs of each type of blouse (with its special twists and turns) are necessary. The learning consideration calls for product specialization. On the other hand, buyers find it convenient to order several garment types from one producer in order to reduce their transaction costs. This leads to expansion through greater product variety.[4] Thus even in garments there are economies of scale, which are partly technological and partly based on marketing requirements. Such scale economies give considerable advantage to the first entrant into a particular market.

In seeking the reasons for relative Philippine stagnation in world markets, then, we are led to three crucial factors. The first reason is considerable difference in the type of foreign involvement in the industry. China, for example, is rapidly absorbing the benefits of a quarter-century of human and organizational learning in Hong Kong. Given the imminent reality of political absorption, those Hong Kong entrepreneurs who intend to remain in China must make their accommodation with the system. American and Japanese investors in Philippines have had far less interest in learning-related investments.

The second reason, which is related to the first point, is the proximity of the apparel industry in China and the East Asian NICs to domestic sources of cheap, high-quality fabric. This gives local enterprises a capability for movement into quality- and time-sensitive garment lines which is simply unavailable to Philippine firms.

Finally, it is quite possible that Philippines' East Asian competitors have simply enjoyed an important first-mover advantage in this market. As noted previously, there seem to be critical minimum scale economies in marketing which the NICs have attained. Beyond a certain sales volume, their suppliers have found it profitable to supplant foreign marketing agents with their own sales arms. Their competitive status and ability to move into higher-quality markets has thereby been enhanced.

In this comparison, then, we see familiar themes recur. For Philippines' competitors, political power translated into deferential quota treatment; as volume and variety expanded, crucial forms of learning were promoted; the availability of cheap, high-quality domestic fabrics turned out to be crucial for movement into more profitable, time-sensitive markets; and capital was mobilized to turn first-mover advantage into marketing expertise as critical minimum scale was attained.

At this stage, then, the case of Philippine stagnation in garments suggests that some opportunities, once lost, may never be regained. Having lost the opportunity in the 1970s to become a major garment exporter, Philippines today faces a much more protectionist environment. Past methods for circumventing quota restrictions have been neutralized by new restrictions; the EEC has been extremely tough in negotiating bilateral agreements since 1977; and protectionist sentiment in the US is clearly on the rise, as evidenced by near-passage of the Jenkins Bill. Behind protective barriers in the US, Japan, and Europe, automated manufacturing methods are starting down the learning curve in precisely those basic apparel lines where Philippines has had significant market presence. Under the circumstances, it is entirely possible that Philippines should simply look elsewhere for sources of competitive advantage.

POLITICAL RESPONSE: TRADE LIMITATION

The two principal markets for developing country clothing exports, the United States and the European Community, have steadily increased their degree of domestic protection. Since 1977, however, relative failure to promote domestic employment has caused Europe to become much more protectionist than the United States. Protection has generally taken the form of "orderly marketing arrangements (OMA)" or "voluntary export restraints (VER)".[5] The appeal of these instruments seems to be largely political. VERs are relatively easy to administer; they allow for simultaneous appeasement of domestic industry and dispensation of rents to allies and countries with large markets for exports.

In the post-war period, the first formal restriction was focused mainly on Japanese cotton goods and was embodied in the Short Term Cotton Textile Arrangement (STA), which went into effect for one year starting on 1 October 1961. Thereafter, country and commodity coverage has increased steadily through the Long Term Arrangement on Cotton Textiles (1962–75) and the Multifiber Arrangement (MFA), which came into effect on 1 January 1974 and has been twice extended, first in 1977 and again in 1981.[6]

The MFA provides an alternative framework to the General Agreement on Tariffs and Trade (GATT) for conducting trade in textiles and clothing. However, it violates GATT's principle of "non-discrimination" (or equal treatment of trading partners). Under the MFA, the US and the EEC negotiate bilateral agreements with individual countries. These agreements limit the amount that can be exported (either by product category, or by some global measure, or both). The agreements also decide on the degree of "flexibility" in these restraints. In addition, the exporting countries face tariffs.[7]

Given the lack of international rules, one can only speculate on the future evolution of quota allocations. For the most part, the "successful" countries have been rewarded by the allocation of ever larger quotas. There is unfortunately an identification problem here. David Yoffie (1983) has argued that the successful countries, particularly South Korea and Taiwan, have been better negotiators and "better cheaters". As noted previously, the recent entry of China as a major force in the world textile and clothing market is partially explained by its geopolitical situation and its ability to offer potentially large markets.

Besides the quantitative limits, each country negotiates flexibility criteria that allow it to go beyond the limits specified; also, for some newly-emerging exporters only a limited number of garments come under restraint. It is clear that only four countries – Hong Kong, Korea, Taiwan and China – have benefitted significantly from relaxation of import restraints. The first three already had high limits in 1981. China has enjoyed a spectacular increase, having increased its quota limit by more than 10 times in 5 years to become the third largest quota holder after Taiwan and Korea. It should be noted that in 1981, the Chinese quota was significantly smaller than the Philippine quota while by 1985 it was three times as large. Another country which has enjoyed very rapid quota growth is Indonesia, though its quota continues to be relatively small. India, Thailand and Haiti actually lost quota between 1982 and 1985.

A recent GATT report provides the basis for an international comparison of quota utilization rates between 1979 and 1982. From this one observes that Philippines has had the lowest quota utilization rates among all major Asian producers (including recent entrants such as Thailand and Indonesia). The trade weighted average utilization rate for Philippines was between 65 and 70 per cent in the early 1980s, somewhat higher for Thailand and Indonesia, and in the range of 90 to 110 per cent for Korea, Taiwan and Hong Kong.[8]

Some care needs to be exercised in interpreting the shortfall in Philippine quota utilization. In 1984 and 1985, for example, Philippines was unable to utilize over $350 million of quota, which equaled more than 50 per cent of the value of exports in those years. However, in some product categories Philippines has utilized a substantial portion (75 per cent or more) of its quota. These include some children's garments, coats, non-knit shirts, and underwear. At the other extreme, Philippines has large unused quotas in floor coverings, woven fabrics and specialty fabrics. In such products

Philippines does not even have the pretense of a production capacity.

Asian exporters have clearly differed significantly in the degree to which they have successfully exploited this system of trade control. We have discussed above the role of institutional interests, marketing strengths, learning, and economies of scale. To complete the picture, we must consider the role of internal quota allocation. Once a quota has been allocated to a country, the national authority has to divide it among domestic firms. The ideal domestic quota allocation system should maximize export earnings, ensuring at the same time that resources are used in the most efficient manner. Assuming that under conditions of no restraint the country would export a greater value than under the restraint, the quota allocation system should ensure that at least the restrained levels are achieved. Under the current system of physical quantity limits, there is the further question whether export of higher valued products should be encouraged.

In a world of perfect information and profit maximizing capitalists, all operating at equal efficiencies, it should not matter who gets the quotas. Everyone will have the same opportunity and capability; in maximizing private profits, the firms will maximize the country's exports. Quota allocation becomes important when some firms have better market information than others. It becomes more important when some firms are satisficers and are content with some minimum level of rent derived from the allocated quota.

In practice it is unlikely that the firms with the best market information will also be profit maximizers. In fact, firms that develop market information and hence export earnings may tend to become satisficers. If the system of quota allocation is such that the "performers", who have the best market information, are continuously under threat of losing quota (in the hope that this will induce them to maximize their export earnings), the actual effect may be perverse: these firms may reduce their investment in generating market information. In a practical sense, therefore, the system of quota allocation must have some degree of stability in order to allow firms to have a relatively long time horizon. Most countries have imparted this stability by rewarding performers. Continued fulfillment of a high percentage allows retention of the quota.

A firm is normally awarded a quota for the year. During the year, the firm may decide that it will be unable to fulfill the quota. In that case a method should be available to transfer the quota to another firm that has the prospect of exporting. The quota may be surrendered to the government and reallocated. Alternatively, it may be sold. The alternative of selling avoids two problems. In most countries, surrender and non-fulfillment of the quota carry penalties; thus the firm holding the quota may choose to produce low-valued items or use resources inefficiently in order to fill its quota. Secondly, if the firm holding the quota is less efficient than the one demanding it, then overall resource use is improved through sale. Most countries, however, also have a penalty for excessive sale (for example, if quota is sold for two consecutive years, then a portion of the sold quota is confiscated); hence there will generally be a disincentive also to sell.

The sale of quotas may not be desirable when firms have similar patterns of resource use and the receipt of export orders is stochastic, favoring different sets of firms from year to year. If the quota were sold in such circumstances, then the supply curve of the quota receiving firm would move inwards and the extent of exports would decline. Mitigating this, however, would be the possibility that the buying firm would be induced to move upscale: since the quota is determined in physical quantities, the price of the quota is also for a physical quantity; once a fixed sum of money has been paid for that unit of quota, then there is an incentive to produce a higher valued good.

The relative importance of the influences described in the preceding paragraphs varies greatly from country to country, depending on the structural constraints to resource mobility, the general business environment and the history of evolution of the industry. Given the complexities involved in evaluating the marginal responses, it is not surprising that all major Asian garment exporters have virtually the same set of rules governing internal quota allocation.[9] Hong Kong and Korea have a somewhat different set of rules from the others; however, the working of the system in Korea is no different from that in the other countries. And although Hong Kong is usually cited as exceptional in that it permits sale of quota, it should be noted that Philippines had a very similar system until 1986. Moreover, even in Hong Kong, initial quota allocation is made on the basis of export performance; there are penalties for non-fulfillment similar to those of other countries; and excessive sale is punished through reduction in quotas.

Although bilateral quota arrangements have been crucial to competitive dynamics in Asia during the past decade, it should be noted that a major change in the prevailing system might well occur in the near future. Its huge current account deficit may be moving the US toward political action on the quota front. For the first time, the replacement of the current quota allocation system with auctioning of quotas to US-based import firms is under active discussion in the US Congress. In 1987, Senator Max Baucas (D-Montana) plans to introduce a bill proposing that auctions be tried out in the next three cases in which the US imposes temporary import quotas. Thus far, only two countries – Australia and New Zealand – have such auctions. In the proposed US system, there would be an active secondary market in quota tickets. C. Fred Bergsten, Director of the Institute for International Economics, has estimated that generalized quota auctions might bring in revenues as high as $7 billion a year.

If such a quota auction system were to replace the current allocation mechanism, the impact on the East Asian NICs would be immediate and probably rather drastic. Korea, Hong Kong, and Taiwan would simply be unable to compete with the new low-wage entrants in the production of many basic lines of apparel and textile products. Asian production generally would become more labor intensive, and employment benefits in the poor countries would rise as profits in the NICs fell. It is difficult to resist the argument that this shift would be progressive for Asia generally. Over the next ten years, the enhanced competition would deliver a Schumpeterian shock to the NICs which would force them to move at greater speed toward the more technology-and capital-intensive lines in which they have been developing competitive advantage. For India, China, Indonesia, Bangladesh, and other states with massive youthful populations, the benefits of expanded employment opportunities in an entry-level industry need not be elaborated upon.

Unfortunately, this scenario cannot be painted in entirely rosy colors. For while a generalized quota auction would have a progressive impact on Asia, it would also preserve the basic barrier – the quota itself – behind which a new force is gathering steam. A decade after the microprocessor first assumed commercial importance, low-cost automated systems for apparel and textile production are beginning to emerge from the development laboratories. Unobtrusively, they are beginning to make their presence felt on the factory floor in the West. A new infant industry is being born, and it will mature progressively behind steep protective walls. Before long, the infant may turn into a world-class competitor which will rock garment production in Asia to its foundations. To this critical subject we now turn our attention.

TECHNOLOGICAL RESPONSE: AUTOMATION AND COMMUNICATIONS

In both textile and garment production, the potential for automation has rapidly increased in recent years. In the introduction to this book, the description of night operations at a fully-automated textile mill in Japan provides one striking illustration of the current potential. The economically-important characteristics of the new technologies may be described as follows:

1. The cost of capital equipment is rising rapidly.
2. Labor input (for given output) is declining sharply.
3. Operators are becoming less skilled on average.
4. The training period of operators is therefore becoming shorter.
5. While operator skills are declining, new skills requiring software and hardware development and maintenance are becoming important.
6. Product quality and production efficiency are increasing; by production efficiency we mean: better use of materials, less work in progress and fewer rejects.

Synthetic Textiles

Synthetic textile production has aspects of both continuous flow and batch processing. Polymerization, at the "upstream" end, is a continuous-flow process which has always been relatively highly automated. Current automation efforts in spinning are also highly advanced. Equipment in advanced installations includes automatic winding equipment capable of reversal and break-repair; robotic mounting and dismounting of spindles; and automatic transfer to automated final packaging. Plant cleaning and interstation transfers are performed by robots. Most of the elements for fully-automated production are in place, and industry specialists foresee the challenge of the next half-decade as lying in fully computer-integrated manufacturing (CIM). The most automated spinning operations in Japan and the US will be characterized by combined office-factory automation and near-"paperless" operations.

The potential for weaving operations is also quite advanced. Robotic interstation transfer is now possible. Existing water-jet loom systems are already so automated that a ratio of 25 high-capacity looms per worker has been realized. Some specialty firms are now using computer-controlled vision systems which automatically inspect huge fabric volumes, marking any defect areas. Again, the automation of separate components of the system is will-nigh complete, and CIM systems will represent the next stage of progress.

Garments

In garment production, the major microelectronics based technological improvements have occurred in pre-assembly (design, marking, grading and cutting) and post-assembly (warehouse management and distribution). The assembly, or sewing, stage has until recently proven relatively resistant to the introduction of microelectronics. Emerging trends are as follows:

Flexibility

A major focus of current effort is on increasing the flexibility of machines. Garment making robots are one example of this move towards flexibility. The following robot characteristics are being sought (Clarke, 1984, p. 210):
1. The ability to recognize arbitrarily shaped pieces.
2. The ability to pick up pieces in a controlled manner.
3. The ability to align fabrics.
4. The ability to sense the need for and take preventive action during the sewing process.

Sequential operations

The most difficult part of automation has turned out to be the transfer of semi-finished output from one workstation to another. The precision required in positioning the workpiece on the new workstation is very high. It is easier to build dedicated transfer lines than to build lines that can continuously adjust to varying workpieces. Vision systems are being designed to monitor the movement of the workpiece along the transfer line and to position it precisely for operation by the next workstation. Such development is rapidly taking place but is not yet commonly in use. In the case of fabrics, there is the additional factor that the material being transferred is limp, so that maintaining the shape of the material during the transfer process is difficult.

One approach to sequential processing is being developed at Textile/Clothing Technology Corporation, commonly referred to as (TC)^2 and an affiliate of the renowned Charles Stark Draper Laboratory in Cambridge, Massachussetts. The project, which is being funded by some US firms and the Amalgamated Clothing and Textile Workers Union, has focused on the design and prototyping of a machine that performs sequential stitching operations. This is possibly the first of its kind, although something like it may be under development in Europe.

The machine, which is now undergoing factory trials, is a set of three or four workstations that sew the sleeve of a suit. The sewing is not a one shot affair. It involves a complex process, referred to as differential sewing: The sewing of a suit sleeve is not done in a straight line but rather in discrete parts, each requiring a different stitching pattern. The workstations are designed to perform particular subtasks, and the transfer mechanism transports the workpiece from one workstation to another.

The cost of such a prototype system is likely to approach $100,000 per worker, although it is clear that this cost will fall sharply once volume production begins. The high capital-labor ratio is sought to be compensated by: (a) reduced skill requirements of the workers, (b) continuous use of the machine, and (c) reduced need to rebundle the pieces of cloth being worked upon in between two operations. Existing systems for the automated manufacture of dress shirts require an investment of $40,000 per worker.

UPS System

A major materials-handling system, referred to as the unit production system (UPS), is likely to spread in the next few years. At present, sewing machine operators spend about 60 per cent of their time handling material. The work pieces are brought to the operator in a large bundle, which she unties, processes and rebundles for the next operator. The new computer-controlled overhead system will bring individual pieces to the operator on a conveyer, thus reducing the time required for unbundling and bundling (see Government of Australia, 1985).

Advanced Technology: The Labor-Saving Potential

In both textile and garment production, the advanced technologies which we have described above are still so costly that they are optimal only in high labor cost environments. Their direct labor-saving potential is illustrated in Table 2.1, which provides estimates of direct labor input for three stylized technologies. The Manual technology represents the state of technology before the advent of microelectro-

TABLE 2.1 *Labor requirements in garment manufacture: women's high style printed polyester dress (number of workers)*

Technology	Manual	Semi-Automated	Robotic
I. Pre assembly (1200 dresses/day)			
Operators	19	10	4
Technicians	4	4	4
Engineers	0	1	1
Overhead workers	1	1	1
II. Assembly (1200 dresses/day)			
Operators	65	35	14
Technicians	1	1	1
Engineers	0	1	1
Overhead workers	4	2	1
III. Post-assembly (1200 dresses/day)			
Operators	12	7	4
Technicians	1	1	1
Engineers	0	1	1
Overhead workers	1	1	1

SOURCES: Interviews; industry publications; garment costing model provided by E.I. DuPont et Nemours, Inc.

nics; Semi-Automated technology incorporates some microelectronics *in individual work stations*. Robotic technology is partially futuristic in the sense that it has yet to be incorporated in production systems. Our view of the Robotic technology has been based on engineering assessments of technologies which are expected to be implemented within the next decade.

We quantify the degree of labor-saving in production by breaking the process down into three steps:

1. *Pre-Assembly*: Grading; marking; cutting. In these three steps, the designs for garment pieces are translated to alternative sizes, laid down on fabric, and the pieces cut out.
2. *Assembly*: The pieces are sewn together and various attachments (buttons, zippers, etc.) are added.

3. *Post-Assembly*: The sewn garments are finished (wrinkles removed, etc.), inspected, and prepared for shipment.

Table 2.1 provides information on reduction in labor input as the technology moves towards greater automation. The number of operators is approximately halved at each move (from Manual to Semi-Automated and from Semi-Automated to Robotic). There is no increase in any other category except a very small increase in the number of engineers. As the detailed presentation of our computer model will make clear, the current cost of Robotic technology is such that adoption is justifiable only in the industrial economies. As we will see, however, the Semi-Automated technology is viable at very low wages. The employment implications for unskilled operators are clearly worrisome.

Advanced Technology: The Time-Saving Potential

In the US, the initial response to the competitive onslaught of low wage countries was that labor content should be reduced. It has since been realized, however, that large gains can be obtained through speeding up the process of production. In describing the major strategic variables which can be influenced by the new technology, Guy Gunzberg, Corporate Vice-President at Hartmarx Corp., recently said: "The *first*, and by far the most important, is time. . . By using technology to shorten the production cycle dramatically, apparel companies can reduce their fashion risks while improving their ability to deliver quality customer service. The *second* strategic variable which technology can affect, of course, is the cost of manufacturing" (*Bobbin*, July 1985, p. 44). There is some reason to be cautious in assessing the importance of reduction in time costs. Nevertheless, it should be noted that by shortening the production cycle two advantages are gained: (a) there is a fall in the cost of working capital and (b) there is a competitive advantage gained through the ability to respond quickly to customer demands.

The longer the material is in the manufacturing or distribution pipeline, the greater the working capital costs. The two ways of reducing the working capital requirements are: (a) reduction of material input through more efficient processing and (b) reduction of processing and distribution time. Computer assisted production can help both in conserving the material and in speeding up production. Some estimates of potential reduction in the length of the production cycle have been provided by Robert Frazier of Kurt Salmon Associates. The current typical length of the inventory pipeline is 66 weeks.

That includes 19 weeks at retail, 24 weeks at apparel, and 23 weeks at the textile and fiber stages. Of this total, only 11 weeks are spent as work-in-progress – when something is actually being done to turn fiber into a finished garment ready for sale. The balance of the 66 weeks – 83% of the total cycle time – is spent in inventory. The fibers, fabrics, or finished garments are waiting for something to happen – waiting to be ordered out of stock, waiting to be shipped, waiting to be packaged or ticketed, and waiting for the customer to buy. This total block of time is our major enemy and has to be reduced. (Frazier, 1985, p. 2).

Microelectronics based technology has the capability to simultaneously reduce labor input and work-in-progress. Frazier forsees the possibility of reducing the cycle time from 66 to 20 weeks. According to Frazier, the most relevant areas for technological progress in garments are: (1) computer design; (2) automatic cutting; (3) flexible sewing and finishing technology incorporating microprocessors; (4) robotic handling; (5) unit production systems; (6) shop-floor controls; (7) logistics; (8) supplier linkage; (9) retail linkage and merchandise control; and (10) implementation.

Another consideration is the need to respond to customer demand at very short notice. If the demand is not met, the entire value of the product is subject to significant depreciation. The importance of this consideration has increased on account of greater competition among producers, which in turn has allowed retailers to become more demanding.[10] The retailer can incur significant losses by carrying an excess of goods that are not selling or by not having in stock something that is in demand. Since the accuracy of the demand forecast improves as the selling season approaches, the retailer naturally values short supply lines. When competing producers are able to offer the same price, the speed of response to retailer demands becomes important; in some situations, retailers are willing to pay higher prices for their purchases in return for a "quick response" from the producer.

The importance of quick response to customer needs is difficult to quantify. A recent study by the Boston Consulting Group (1985) indicates that the problem of accurate demand forecasting is important for products such as men's casual shirts, women's blouses and women's skirts, all of which have short selling seasons.

ORGANIZATIONAL RESPONSE: INDUSTRY RESTRUCTURING

A major factor influencing the pace of technical change in the West has been the predominance of very small scale firms in the apparel industry. In the US, for example, there are about 35 000 textile-related firms, of which the majority are small apparel firms. For these small firms, the cost of an automated response to the Asian challenge is simply prohibitive.

When the apparel has been standardized (such as in jeans or men's underwear), large firms using dedicated machines have emerged. In a few garment lines, then, US firms have already used automated systems to compete on a more even footing with the NICs. However, the bulk of apparel products are subject to rapid variation in style, color, etc. This requires the production of small sized lots and the ability to respond quickly to changing demand. Machinery with such flexibility was not available till recently; indeed, from our interviews and reading of trade journals, it appears that only a limited degree of flexibility is possible even with the most recent technology.[11] As a consequence, small firms, which use very little fixed equipment and rely mainly on their labor, have remained the predominant form of organization. The labor is, in theory, programmable.

As competitive pressure increases, however, there is evidence of increasing concentration in the textile and apparel industry. Hoffman and Rush (1985) have concluded:

> There is now a strong feeling within the clothing industry that this process of concentration will continue and indeed possibly pick up pace in the future. One recent analysis of these trends has concluded that "continued growth – even survival – is not assured for the great bulk of all apparel manufacturers – the small and medium company." This study suggests the possibility that by the end of the century only 75 to 100 manufacturers will account for 75 per cent of sales. This view was strongly reflected in our interviews. Most of the larger firms felt that the trend towards increasing concentration was inevitable. They believed that medium-sized firms too small to reap economies of scale or undertake large

capital investments and too large to be very flexible would decline in numbers. These would be replaced by a greater number of large firms and a viable but greatly diminished group of small firms which would continue to survive on the basis of their flexibility. (Hoffman/Rush, ch. 7).

The economies of scale they refer to are those being generated by the new technology. As was indicated above, the cost of new capital equipment has been steadily rising. The new technology has, however, had only limited success in achieving flexibility. "If a machine is designed to be ultra-flexible, then almost certainly the cost increases. Therefore, a compromise is sought that has generally resulted in machines with limited flexibility" (Clarke, 1984, p. 208).

A reflection of the trade-off between economies of scale and flexibility has been the increasing tendency to specialize in narrow product ranges. Hoffman and Rush (1985, ch. 7) point out: "Many firms have narrowed their product mix and chosen to specialize in particular sub-sectors such as lingerie or mens and boys outerwear. At the same time larger firms have expanded the scale of their operations (after absorbing smaller firms) to a level that allows them to achieve internationally competitive production runs."

A very similar phenomenon is taking place in the textile industry. *The Wall Street Journal* recently reported: "Unable to stem the wave of inexpensive foreign fabric imports, U.S. textile companies are rapidly combining to stake out market positions they can defend." The combinations have mainly been towards increased specialization to dominate particular segments of the market. "The rule used to be: Make all kinds of textiles – apparel and industrial fabric, and domestic goods – so 'if one was weak they could make it up in the other two,' says Freddie H. Wood, senior vice president of Kurt Salmon Associates, an Atlanta-based consulting firm. 'Now the thing to do is focus'" (*The Wall Street Journal*, 5 February 1986, p. 6).[12]

As we noted previously, increasing concentration is likely to enhance the political power of textile and garment firms. Since their interests are partially antagonistic, however, it is not clear how this increased power would affect the existing level of protection in the US. For optimal technology choice in the US, the implications of this restructuring are ambiguous. One interpretation has been that the growth in firm size will speed up the process of technical change in the garment and textile industries. And undoubtedly this will happen. However, the industry itself has its eyes also on higher profits that will become possible as the number of players decreases, and hence as the market power of the survivors increases. By combining and grabbing a big share of the market, mills hope to stabilize prices. "The textile industry has been plagued with dog-eat-dog competition for years," says Maurice Fishman, senior vice president of Guildford Mills Inc., Greensboro, N.C. "By controlling a market, it may be possible to get a more equitable return on investment" (*The Wall Street Journal*, 5 February, 1986, p. 6).

MODELLING COSTS IN GARMENT AND TEXTILE PRODUCTION

As the preceding discussion has suggested, realistic depiction of international competitive dynamics in textile and garment production requires a relatively complex model. While we have not included the political and organizational factors, we have attempted to study the technological complexity at a high level of detail. Our approach treats textile production as a nationally-integrated operation and uses the results as a basis for determining relative fabric input costs for garment production. Our textile cost model is similar to the models for semiconductor and automobile production which will be presented in the following chapters. For garments, our modeling approach allows for several additional complications:

Alternative sites/technologies in multistage production

As noted previously, garment production can be conceptually divided into three categories: pre-assembly (patterning, grading, marking); assembly (sewing); and post-assembly (finishing, inspection, packing). In many cases, these three production steps are accomplished in different countries. Each production step can also be performed at varying levels of labor intensity. Our model therefore evaluates competitive costs at each stage of production for alternative production sites and technologies.

Time accounting

The model also takes account of the fact that garment competition is affected by the time involved in order-delivery cycles. Alternative garment production technologies have very different throughput rates, and transit times between countries differ substantially.[13]

Inventory-related interest costs must also be considered, since buffer stocks accumulate at each stage of the production process. One of the major goals of production planners in the US is a drastic reduction in buffer stocks through electronic coordination of ordering and production. Such coordination is only likely to be feasible for domestic operations in the near future, and it may provide a major source of competitive advantage for US producers. Our model includes a time accounting system which takes these factors into account. It tracks the time which accumulates during production and transit, and estimates the associated inventory costs.

Product diversity

Garments differ greatly in their quality, complexity and ease of assembly. A careful analysis of garment production therefore requires the consideration of a variety of product types. For this study, we have chosen six garments whose differences in production economics are reflected in widely differing levels of import penetration in the US market. The garments chosen for study are:
1. Men's slacks.
2. Men's single-needle long sleeve dress shirt.
3. Men's high style knit pullover shirt.
4. Women's high style printed polyester dress.
5. Women's high style printed skirt.
6. Women's low style knit pullover shirt.

The Data Base

The data requirements for the textile/garment model are obviously considerable. We have constructed estimates of alternative technologies for three stages of textile production. In addition, we have specified three-stage production technologies for the six garment products listed above. Tables A.2.1–7 (in Appendix 2) include our technology data, by product and stage of production. We have also estimated throughput times by stage of production; buffer stock delays; transport costs for air and sea shipment; and associated transport times. Our model contains estimates of the relevant input cost data by production site. Finally, we have obtained product-specific tariff rates, and incorporated these in a way which reflects the application of US 807 tariff regulations to multi-stage production.[14]

Textile production technologies

Table A.2.1 (in Appendix 2) specifies the technology data for three-stage production of a synthetic-based fabric. At the Spinning stage, automation has progressed quite rapidly. In the transition from Manual to Semi-Automated technology, tremendous labor saving is possible with little more than a doubling of capital costs. This industry is not far from realizing Robotic technology in essentially "workerless" spinning operations. Additional capital costs will be substantial ($1 million), but not overwhelming in a relative sense. [15] Anticipated increments in associated engineer/technician services are also relatively modest. Similar patterns of capital–labor substitution and relative cost apply to the Preparation and Weaving phases of textile production.

Although learning does not seem to play as central a role in textiles as in other sectors we have studied, we include estimates of initial and final load factors.[16] In addition, we recognize that advanced technologies require a more substantial investment in learning than their labor-intensive counterparts. We therefore incorporate estimates of the additional costs incurred in learning (labeled Standard Learning Investment (%) in Table A.2.1). These are calculated as a percentage of the wage bill for technicians, engineers, and overhead personnel. We also estimate standard learning time, which is the number of years required for transition from initial to final load factors in production. Since the estimated difference in load factors is very small for textiles, learning time is not very important in this particular model.

Garment Production Technologies (Appendix 2: Tables A.2.2–7)

Pre-assembly

As previously noted, Pre-Assembly consists of grading, marking, and cutting the fabric prior to sewing. Much of Pre-Assembly has been automated in existing "best practice" OECD plants, and the major transition in capital requirements is therefore from Manual to Semi-Automated technology. Pre-Assembly work is more skill-intensive than most fabric production operations, and the labor input requirements reflect this difference. In the transition from Manual to Robotic technology, labor input is approximately halved at each step. By comparison with technology transitions in textiles, this labor-saving is relatively modest. In absolute terms, however, the labor requirements for Pre-Assembly are themselves relatively modest.

It is important to note the production scale which characterizes our Pre-Assembly technology specifications. Pre-Assembly capacity is 12 000 units per day, while for Assembly and Post-Assembly we use 1200 units per day as the standard. There are clearly economies of scale in Pre-Assembly.[17] Because of the interaction between skill requirements and technology, we posit substantial learning possibilities for all three Pre-Assembly technologies. Learning in Manual Pre-Assembly is embodied in the people who grade, mark, and cut the fabric. With the transition through Semi-Automated to Robotic technology, the associated skill is increasingly embodied in the machines themselves. The learning effects of technology transition are threefold. At start-up, advanced technologies cannot be smoothly operated, and initial load factors are therefore low. However, most of the difficult skills are now embodied in the equipment, and the standard learning time is considerably lower than for Manual technology. There is some difference in the final load factor as well, since wastage rates are lower for automated Pre-Assembly. Finally, it is worth noting that throughput time declines very substantially with the transition to higher technologies. The reason is obvious: computer-aided equipment can move through the Pre-Assembly steps at speeds which simply overwhelm the best efforts of skilled human operators.

Assembly

Garment assembly reveals a very different pattern of trade-offs in technology switching. The major jump in capital costs comes in the transition from Semi-Automated to Robotic technology. Semi-Automated plants employ microprocessor-assisted sewing equipment but leave the movement and positioning of fabric itself to the operators. These latter operations have proven extremely difficult to automate, and much recent research and development has focused on them. It is clear that equipment which can almost fully replace human labor in sewing is going to be enormously expensive for some time to come. With Robotic production, the cost of capital per worker will escalate into the range which has long prevailed in the automobile industry.

Even with Robotic sewing technology, the degree of labor saving will not match current possibilities in textile production. Operators should decline approximately 80 per cent in the transition from

Manual to Robotic technology. A slight increase in associated technical labor is expected. In addition, a modest improvement in standard learning time can be anticipated. This improvement is far below that for Pre-Assembly because sewing does not require the sort of extended learning period which has historically characterized patterning, grading, and marking.

In two major respects, however, the transition to Robotics in Assembly and Pre-Assembly has similar implications. In Assembly, the initial load factor is also expected to be quite low. Again, however, there is a major compensating factor. Robotic garment assembly will incorporate Unit Production Systems (UPS), which eliminate the bundling now used to transport pieces between sewing stations.[18] This innovation, coupled with the speed and accuracy of Robotic positioning and sewing equipment, will drastically reduce throughput time. After a modest drop from 25 to 20 days in the transition from Manual to Semi-Automated production, throughput time plunges to 5 days with Robotic production.

Post-assembly

The patterns of Post-Assembly technology switching are generally intermediate between those of the other two stages. Semi-Automated finishing processes are already relatively capital-intensive, and the transition to Robotic processes is not anticipated to require the jump in investment which will be associated with the transition to Robotic Assembly. Nevertheless, Post-Assembly is currently lagging behind Pre-Assembly in degree of capital intensity. At least a three-fold increase in investment will be required for fully automated finishing.

Input Costs

Dynamic competition in the textile/garment sector presents a fascinating puzzle because production stages are so easily scattered among different sites. In order to capture the essence of this complexity, we have simulated outcomes for combinations of four sites: Korea, the US, China, and Jamaica. Appendix 2, Table A.2.8 includes the relevant input cost numbers for the four countries, along with anticipated change rates. Among the major patterns in the data, the most striking is the huge disparity in wages. Basic ratios relating US and Korean wages to those for the Chinese are approximately 20:1 and 3:1, respectively. For textiles and garments, we posit high wage growth rates for both Korea and China.

Model Operations

There are basically four variables in the modeling system: Production stage; production technology; production site; and mode of transportation between sites. In principal, production can take place under all possible combinations of values for these variables. In our model, there are 3 technologies per production stage, 3 production stages, 2 modes of transport between site (air and sea), and an arbitrary number of sites. For even a modest number of sites, the number of combinations which must be considered mounts into the hundreds. As the number of sites expands, the number of combinations grows quickly into the tens of thousands. For present purposes, we have therefore limited our consideration to four sites.

Least-Cost Technology Selection: Synthetic Textiles

The first stage in model operations is the determination of least-cost technologies by processing stage and production site. Differing startup dates can be specified for alternative technologies. Among those technologies which are operational in each period, the least-cost mode is chosen for subsequent calculations. In the textile case, for example, typical model output for Spinning, Preparation, and Weaving can be found in Table 2.2. The simulation begins during the present period and calculates comparative unit costs for six years into the future. Korea and Jamaica are constrained from beginning Semi-Automated production until the third simulation year, and Robotic production at both sites is ruled out. China is allowed to begin Semi-Automated production in the fifth year, and Robotic production is ruled out. The US is allowed Semi-Automated production in the first year, but Robotic production does not begin until the fourth simulation year.

The results show that the startup constraints have economic consequences only for the US. For Korean Spinning, Preparation, and Weaving, the Manual technology remains optimal throughout the simulation period. For Jamaica and China, the same thing is true. In the US case, however, Robotic production turns out to be optimal as soon as it becomes available.

The next stage of model operation for textiles is straightforward. Since textile production is modeled as a country-specific integrated operation, site-specific production costs are obtained by simple addition of stage-specific costs. Transport costs to the US are added

TABLE 2.2   *Unit costs (US$) for textile production*

Year		1987	1988	1989	1990	1991	1992
Spinning							
Korea	[L]	0.7	0.72	0.74	0.77	0.79	0.82
	[M]	–	–	0.81	0.82	0.82	0.82
	[H]	–	–	–	–	–	–
U.S.	[L]	2.06	2.17	2.3	2.44	2.58	2.75
	[M]	1.02	1.04	1.07	1.09	1.11	1.15
	[H]	–	–	–	0.94	0.94	0.96
Jamaica							
	[L]	0.81	0.83	0.84	0.85	0.87	0.88
	[M]	–	–	0.95	0.95	0.95	0.95
	[H]	–	–	–	–	–	–
China	[L]	0.58	0.59	0.6	0.61	0.62	0.63
	[M]	–	–	–	–	0.82	0.82
	[H]	–	–	–	–	–	–
Preparation							
Korea	[L]	0.06	0.06	0.06	0.06	0.07	0.07
	[M]	–	–	0.08	0.08	0.09	0.09
	[H]	–	–	–	–	–	–
U.S.	[L]	0.19	0.21	0.22	0.23	0.25	0.27
	[M]	0.13	0.14	0.14	0.14	0.15	0.16
	[H]	–	–	–	0.1	0.1	0.11
Jamaica	[L]	0.06	0.06	0.06	0.06	0.06	0.07
	[M]	–	–	0.09	0.09	0.09	0.09
	[H]	–	–	–	–	–	–
China	[L]	0.04	0.05	0.05	0.05	0.05	0.05
	[M]	–	–	–	–	0.08	0.08
	[H]	–	–	–	–	–	–
Weaving							
Korea	[L]	0.11	0.11	0.11	0.12	0.12	0.13
	[M]	–	–	0.21	0.21	0.21	0.21
	[H]	–	–	–	–	–	–
U.S.	[L]	0.4	0.43	0.45	0.48	0.52	0.55
	[M]	0.26	0.26	0.27	0.28	0.29	0.29
	[H]	–	–	–	0.24	0.24	0.25
Jamaica	[L]	0.12	0.12	0.12	0.13	0.13	0.13
	[M]	–	–	0.23	0.23	0.23	0.23
	[H]	–	–	–	–	–	–
China	[L]	0.08	0.08	0.08	0.08	0.08	0.08
	[M]	–	–	–	–	0.2	0.2
	[H]	–	–	–	–	–	–

NOTE:
[L]   refers to Low (Manual) technology.
[M]   refers to Medium (Semi-Automated) technology.
[H]   refers to High (Robotic) technology.

for non-US producers. The results (Table 2.3) show two major forces at work during the 6-year period. First, rapid wage growth in Korea increases the relative appeal of Jamaica as a textile production site. From a slight cost advantage relative to Jamaica, Korea rises to approximate parity during the simulation. China remains considerably cheaper.

In the US case, the advent of Robotic production in the fourth simulation year has a positive competitive impact. Although US fabrics remain considerably more expensive than their Korean, Chinese, and Jamaican counterparts, they drop substantially in relative cost. The slower growth of US wages also has an ameliorating effect. The US/Korean cost ratio drops from about 1.5 to about 1.3 during the six-year simulation period.

TABLE 2.3   *Unit production costs for least-cost technology combinations: textile production*

	1987	1988	1989	1990	1991	1992
Korea	0.59	0.59	0.60	0.61	0.63	0.64
US	0.87	0.88	0.90	0.80	0.80	0.83
Jamaica	0.62	0.62	0.63	0.64	0.64	0.65
China	0.52	0.53	0.53	0.53	0.53	0.54

Optimal Site/Technology Conbinations: Garments

In the first phase of garment model operations, stage-specific unit costs are calculated for each feasible technology and production site. As before, differing start-up dates can be imposed for alternative technologies. The model then sets up all possible combinations of sites for multi-stage production. First, an evaluation year is selected. Both unit costs and process times associated with optimum Pre-Assembly technologies are recorded. The first set of combinations is then produced by linking Pre-Assembly in all sites to Assembly in all sites. Two modes of transit – air and sea – between sites are allowed for. For each linked pair, a transit cost and transit time are calculated.[19] Finally, US 807 tariff regulations are accounted for. The ultimate destination in this model is the US, and according to US regulations any value added outside the US is subject to the product-specific tariff. The model therefore checks to see whether Pre-

Assembly has taken place in the US. If not, the product-specific tariff rate is applied to value added in Pre-Assembly.

Once the linkage costs and times have been calculated, the model adds the unit cost of the least-cost Assembly technology at each site. The associated process time is also added to the time account. Then another set of pairings is effected. This time, all pairings from the first two stages are combined with all possible production sites for Post-Assembly. Again, transit costs and times for air and sea modes are recorded. If Assembly has not occurred in the US, the product-specific tariff rate is also applied to value added in Assembly in determining cumulative cost.

Finally, the model introduces a routing from all Post-Assembly sites to the US. Once again, transit costs and times are accounted for, as is the application of the tariff to value added in non-US Post-Assembly. The model thus yields a full accounting of cumulative costs, tariff charges, and times elapsed in production and transit. For Robotic production in the US, one further factor is accounted for. Fabric and garment pieces are currently estimated to sit in buffer stocks for a total of 44 weeks. With electronic integration, this buffer time could be reduced to about 20 weeks. The model accounts for this factor with the following rule: If garment Pre-Assembly occurs in the US under Robotic conditions, electronic links are assumed to exist and 20 weeks are added to the total time elapsed in production and transit. For other combinations, 44 weeks are added.

The model is designed in such a way that separable effects can be calculated for production costs, time costs, transport costs, and tariffs. In this way, the workings of dynamic competitive advantage under alternative assumptions can be discerned. In order to illustrate this facility, Table 2.4 presents a series of results for women's high style polyester dresses.

The first entry in Table 2.4 is the ranking of the site combination among 512 alternatives, ordered from least to most costly. The next three entries are the sites for each stage (Pre-Assembly, Assembly and Post-Assembly). Then comes the appropriate calculation of unit cost. Finally, cumulative time in production, transit and inventory is displayed.

Table 2.4a presents ordered results for site combinations without the addition of time-specific interest charges. The fabric used for garment production is assumed to be available to all sites through international markets at current Chinese cost (about 40 per cent below US cost, according to our textile model results). Robotic

TABLE 2.4   *Women's high style printed polyester dress: competitive advantage estimates*

(a) No Tariff, No Time Cost, No Robotic Production

Rank	Pre-Assm.	Assm.	Post-Assm.	Cost	Time
1	Jamaica	Jamaica	Jamaica	4.88	42
5	China	China	China	4.96	67
9	US	Jamaica	Jamaica	5.15	47
11	Korea	Korea	Korea	5.21	66
15	Korea	China	China	5.24	77
33	Korea	Jamaica	Jamaica	5.44	72
35	China	Jamaica	Jamaica	5.44	72
46	US	China	China	5.57	97
73	US	Korea	Korea	5.82	96

(b) No Time Cost, No Robotic Production

Rank	Pre-Assm.	Assm.	Post-Assm.	Cost	Time
1	US	Jamaica	Jamaica	5.38	46
3	US	China	China	5.77	96
11	Jamaica	Jamaica	Jamaica	6.03	41
15	US	Korea	Korea	6.05	96
18	China	China	China	6.09	66
35	Korea	Korea	Korea	6.35	66
39	Korea	China	China	6.36	76
60	Korea	Jamaica	Jamaica	6.58	71
62	China	Jamaica	Jamaica	6.60	71
113	US	US	US	7.03	36

(c) No Robotic Production

Rank	Pre-Assm.	Assm.	Post-Assm.	Cost	Time
1	US	Jamaica	Jamaica	5.54	46
3	US	China	China	5.94	96
11	US	Korea	Korea	6.23	96
17	Jamaica	Jamaica	Jamaica	6.44	41
23	China	China	China	6.50	66
38	Korea	Korea	Korea	6.78	66
42	Korea	China	China	6.78	76
67	Korea	Jamaica	Jamaica	7.02	71
69	China	Jamaica	Jamaica	7.04	71
85	US	US	US	7.18	36

(d) Robotic Production

Rank	Pre-Assm.	Assm.	Post-Assm.	Cost	Time
1	US	Jamaica	Jamaica	5.43	38
3	US	China	China	5.83	88
11	US	Korea	Korea	6.12	88
27	Jamaica	Jamaica	Jamaica	6.44	41
31	China	China	China	6.50	66
37	US	US	US	6.56	10
49	Korea	Korea	Korea	6.78	66
53	Korea	China	China	6.78	76
85	Korea	Jamaica	Jamaica	7.02	71
87	China	Jamaica	Jamaica	7.04	71

production in the US has been precluded. In addition, no tariffs are added. Thus, the Table presents a measure of "pure" competitive advantage in garments production, given currently-available technology. Table entries have been restricted to combinations which are in the top 200 of the 512 possible combinations relevant for this case.

In this "pure" case, least-cost production in the US ranks below 200 – not cost-competitive at all. Integrated operations using low technology in Jamaica and China are least costly (1st and 5th ranked – $4.88 and $4.96, respectively). The combination of US Pre-Assembly with Jamaican Assembly and Post-Assembly is not far behind (9th ranked), at $5.15. Then comes integrated production in Korea (11th ranked), at $5.21. Other combinations (including Pre-Assembly in Korea and subsequent operations in Jamaica) are close competitors.

From the viewpoint of the NICs, two features of these results are significant. First, integrated production in either China or Jamaica is less costly than in Korea. Secondly, the combination of US Pre-Assembly and Jamaican downstream operations is less costly than Korean production, *even when time costs and US tariffs are not taken into account*. From Korea's perspective, things obviously do not improve as the calculation gets more realistic. When US 807 tariff regulations are introduced (Table 2.4b), combinations which include US Pre-Assembly move to the top. The US–Jamaica combination now ranks first, followed somewhat distantly by US–China and even more distantly by US–Korea. Integrated production in Korea falls from 11th to 35th in the rank ordering. Integrated production in the US also appears in the rankings, having risen to 113th from below 200th.

As before, integrated production operations in China and Jamaica produce lower-cost garments than those in Korea. When tariffs are retained and time-related inventory interest charges are included (Table 2.4c), Korea's position deteriorates further.

Combinations with US fabric purchase and Pre-Assembly contine to dominate, and US integrated production advances to 85th ranking. Integrated production in Korea falls a little further, to 38th. Finally, Robotic production in the US is allowed. Fully-integrated US production now jumps to 37th ranking ($6.56) – within striking distance of the only remaining combination which includes Korea. Indeed, when relative elapsed times are taken into account, the remaining unit cost disparity between US–Asian combinations and integrated US production may not be sufficient to outweigh the appeal of the huge US time advantage (10 days vs. 88 days for Korea and China). Integrated production in Korea continues to fall in the rankings, reaching the 49th position. Thus, the model projects that under existing tariff regulations, fully-accounted unit cost in Korean production of women's dresses in this category will be higher than US unit cost with Robotic production.

As currently implemented, then, our dynamic costing model is capable of a relatively sophisticated calculation of competitive advantage for specific garment products. In the case of women's high-style polyester dresses, the advent of Robotic production and a full accounting of costs and times make the US situation relatively favourable. This is particularly true with respect to Korea, and less so for Jamaica and China. For other products, Korea's situation vis-à-vis the US does not appear so unfavourable. Our model results do show unambiguously that the advent of Robotic production in the US, the entry of China into the garment market, and the emerging importance of time costs and time delays have all combined to substantially reduce Korea's competitive advantage in garment production.

THE COMPETITIVE FUTURE IN GARMENTS: A GENERAL FORECAST

We have now provided a detailed introduction to the dynamic competitive advantage model for garments. In this section, we will present a relatively broad set of forecasts for several garment lines. Table 2.5 summarizes our simulation results for six garment products.

TABLE 2.5　Production costs of six garments (in US $)

	Integrated Production for US Market				Cost Accounts	Production Partnerships for US Market			
	China	Korea	US^a	US^b	US^b China	US^b Jamaica	US^b Korea	Korea China	Korea Jamaica
Women's high-quality dress									
No tariff	6.23*	6.60	9.31	—	6.52	6.16**	6.92	6.57	6.77
tariff	7.62	8.07	9.31	—	6.67	6.38**	7.15	7.95	8.22
Women's high-quality skirt									
No tariff	3.78***	4.01	5.67	—	3.92	3.79	4.16	3.94	4.06
tariff	4.65*	4.93	5.67	—	4.01	3.92**	4.30	4.80	4.97
Standard men's slacks									
No tariff	3.27***	3.81	7.48	4.40	3.36	3.61	3.89	3.37	3.81
tariff	4.36*	5.06	7.48	4.40	3.57**	3.96	4.27	4.45	5.05
Standard men's dress shirt									
No tariff	3.50***	3.95	6.75	4.89	3.71	3.74	4.15	3.69	4.03
tariff	4.56*	5.15	6.75	4.89	3.93**	4.09	4.51	4.75	5.22
Men's knit pullover shirt									
No tariff	1.64***	1.93	3.99	2.88	1.85	1.85	2.12	1.77	1.94
tariff	2.25*	2.65	3.99	2.88	2.00**	2.07	2.36	2.38	2.62
Women's knit pullover shirt									
No tariff	1.56***	1.85	3.95	2.89	1.71	1.79	1.97	1.65	1.85
tariff	2.16*	2.56	3.95	2.89	1.84**	2.01	2.21	2.25	2.54
Time Account									
Days in process & transit	75	66	36	10	95	35	88	80	70

* Indicates least-cost integrated producer
** Indicates least-cost production overall
*** Integrated producer with least overall cost
^{a} Production with Semi-Automated technology. This should be understood as current "best practice," not as typical of U.S. firms at present
^{b} Production with Robotic technology

Again, our simulations are based on cost data for one OECD country (the US), an East Asian NIC (Korea), one offshore site near the US (Jamaica) and one low-wage Asian competitor (China). They represent projected "fully accounted" garment costs (with and without existing tariffs) during the coming half-decade, as automated technology becomes available in the US.[20] Our evidence suggests that the combination of OECD automation and new low-wage competition will put great pressure on NIC producers in the next round of world competition. It indicates that low-wage exporters like China can maintain solid growth in apparel exports over the next decade, with high-quality garments holding the greatest promise. They also suggest, however, that even China will be significantly affected by the advent of apparel automation. Chinese producers will encounter increasing competitive pressure from automated domestic producers of standard garment lines in the US, Europe, and Japan. They may therefore have to re-orient their marketing toward the NICs as the latter begin moving out of this sector.

In fully-integrated garment production, China is clearly least-cost in all garment categories. Both Korean and US producers stand at a clear cost disadvantage. This is true whether or not the projected costs for robotic production in the US are considered. For high-quality garments (e.g. women's high-fashion dresses and skirts) where automated sewing is not likely to be feasible for some time, integrated Chinese production is challenged only by some joint production arrangements. The arrangements portrayed in Table 2.5 involve fabric input and automated pre-sewing processes in the US, followed by sewing and finishing at another site. Such arrangements are treated favorably under US law, which taxes only the value added to the process outside the US. The results suggest that US–Chinese and US–Caribbean arrangements[21] are closely matched.

For the four standard garments (slacks, dress shirts, men's and women's knit pullovers), Chinese integrated production or US–Chinese production partnerships are least-cost in all cases. However, with full automation US unit production costs come *much closer* to those of China, and the inclusion of tariffs brings them to near-parity in two cases (men's slacks, men's dress shirts). In all four cases, US–Caribbean partnerships have costs which are quite close to those of Chinese or US–Chinese production.

Of course, the more time-sensitive the product market, the more attractive US–integrated or US–Caribbean production looks. Comparative times in process and transit are also presented in Table 2.5.

For integrated, automated US production, total time in process and transit is only 10 days. This increases to over a month for the US–Caribbean arrangement; to over two months for Chinese and Korean production using less advanced technologies; and to about three months for US–Asian joint production. When associated time in inventories is added, the difference becomes even larger.

To summarize, our results suggest substantial changes in world garment competition during the next decade. First, the days of the NICs seem to be ebbing. Our results show clearly that Korean production in all garment classes will be hit by enhanced competition on both sides. In standard garments, both US robotic production and production in fast-emerging low-cost sites such as China show clear cost superiority. In high-quality garments, production by China or US–Chinese and US–Caribbean partnerships looks highly competitive. Unfortunately, the prospect of declining NIC competitiveness does not imply clear sailing for China and other low-wage states in this industry. In high-quality garments, US–Caribbean partnerships have costs quite comparable with those of Asian producers and substantially shorter response times. In standard garments, low-cost US–Caribbean arrangements will be joined by integrated US firms using robotic technology.

At present, it seems that robotic technology will be sufficiently cost-saving in many standard garment lines to shift the competitive balance back toward the US, Western Europe, and Japan.

If the low-wage states of South and Southeast Asia are to enjoy rapid, as opposed to modest, growth in garment exports, much will depend on policies in Japan and the East Asian NICs. In theory, the low-wage states could play the Caribbean role in production partnerships with Japan or the NICs, and Chinese production will undoubtedly prove particularly attractive to entrepreneurs in Hong Kong. China's economy has obvious problems, however, and there does not seem to be any reason why other states in the area could not profit from joint production arrangements.

CURRENT TRENDS: DO THEY SUPPORT THE FORECAST?

This study is primarily concerned with analyzing the evolution of competitive dynamics in the near future, as Robotic production comes onstream in the US and other OECD countries. In the Western Hemisphere, our modeling results suggest that there will be a shift in the competitive balance back towards sites in the US and the Caribbean. Since some of the technologies which we have discussed are actually being installed at present, it is of interest to examine the current record for a trend in line with the predictions of our model. There is very little good information on current location trends. In a recent survey by Kurt Salmon Associates, a very small sample of US firms was asked about intentions to invest in new capacity. Since the sample was small, the results of this survey have to be viewed very cautiously.

However, within this sample the message is clear. The responses are tabulated in Table 2.6. In 1985, US firms were planning to locate their future capacity expansion either within the US or in the Caribbean. This result is certainly in line with the comparative cost numbers generated by our own modeling exercises.

TABLE 2.6   *Investment location intentions of US producers (number of firms)*

	US	Caribbean	Central America	Far East	Elsewhere
Women's wear	4	1	0	0	1
Men's wear	3	2	0	0	0
Children's wear	3	2	1	0	0
Diversified	1	3	1	0	0
Total	11	8	2	0	0

SOURCE: Kurt Salmon Associates, *Sourcing 1985*

Relocation to the OECD Countries

The above table provides some evidence of intentions to expand capacity within the US. This cannot strictly be considered relocation, in as much as it does not involve closing down offshore locations and re-establishing them in the US. The data do indicate that in the future the tendency to locate outside the American continent is likely to be weaker than in the past. The extent of actual *relocation* is also not very well known. At this stage, in any case, it is probably small. Hoffman and Rush (1985, ch. 8, p. 83) have concluded: "Turning to the issue of *microelectronics induced* trade reversal in the current period, our research uncovered relatively few instances where the use of MRIs (microelectronics related investments) by developed country clothing firms had led them (or the retail sector) to substitute domestically produced for previously imported products. There certainly were examples...but when measured against Third World clothing exports of more than $14,000 million in 1982 they accounted for an insignificant percentage. The areas where there are some indications of trade reversal are: hosiery, jeans, shoes, men's shirts and children's clothes."

More of the trade reversal phenomenon is reported in Europe than in the United States. The Europeans have had wage rates 20-30 per cent higher than in the US and so have had a stronger incentive to automate. The result has been the production of increasingly efficient technologies which permit competition with low wage countries.

The OECD Periphery

The Caribbean

There are clear signs that the Caribbean is becoming an increasingly important site for production aimed at the US market.[22] Investment in garment production is being undertaken by US, Far Eastern and domestic producers. Far Eastern producers are using the Caribbean as a means for getting around their own quota limitations.[23] While there is considerable foreign enthusiasm for investment in the Caribbean and nearby Latin American states, local entrepreneurs are also making a serious effort to be internationally competitive. Recent Bobbin shows (where the latest garment making technology is displayed) have attracted a very large number of Latin American producers. These producers have apparently taken a keen interest in the recent generations of capital equipment (*Bobbin*, November 1985, pp. 122–26).

There are at least four different forces responsible for the move towards the Caribbean:

1. Caribbean wages are very low. Caribbean wage rates are significantly lower than those in Hong Kong, Taiwan, Korea and Singapore. Lower Caribbean wages, however, should not be considered in isolation; they have been low relative to other countries for a long period of time. Yet the movement towards sourcing and production in the Caribbean is a recent phenome-

non. Moreover, the concurrent move to the European periphery cannot be explained by relatively low wages.

2. Another reason frequently cited for production in the Caribbean is the relatively quick turn around possible for US producers because of proximity to the US. This fits in with the reason for locating in the Mediterranean when producing for the European market. In both the US and European cases, the recent development of automated pre-assembly technologies is undoubtedly relevant in this context.

3. A further factor probably is the development of infrastructure that has taken place in the Caribbean over the last decade, making business transactions in the region more convenient and cost effective. There is also a growing feeling that the region is more stable than had been believed.

4. The Caribbean Basin Economy Recovery Act is also providing a general fillip to growth in the region. It provides, among other things, for duty-free entry for a wide range of products. Textiles and apparel are apparently not yet included in that list, although there is some expectation that they will be in the near future. Also, much of the recent growth of apparel production in the Caribbean has been under 807 tariff code auspices: US producers pre-assemble the garment, which is then sewn in the Caribbean. The import duty is levied only on the value added outside the US. Again, 807 strategies have been open for a long time (all offshore semiconductor assembly in the Far East has been done on that basis), so that there does not appear to be a direct causal relationship between 807 provisions and recent location decisions.

North Africa and the European periphery

A similar trend has been observed with reference to the European market: location in North Africa and the "European periphery" (Spain, Portugal, Greece, Turkey) has become increasingly attractive. These trends represent a move away from the Far East, which has dominated developing country textile exports. There also seems to be a focus on specific regions, which in effect means that many countries of Asia, Latin America and Africa which did not participate in the exports of textiles in the 1960s and 1970s are unlikely to do so in the current phase either.

CONCLUSIONS

In this chapter, as elsewhere in the book, we have analyzed technical change using three stylized technologies: Manual, Semi-Automated and Robotic. Our results suggest that in garments, technological progress to date has been such that "Semi-Automated" technology usually overwhelms Manual technology, even in China. Robotic pre- and post-assembly techniques have been coming onstream in the OECD countries, and the technology now exists for automating the sewing of basic garments as well. Since garment production can be broken up into distinct stages, our evidence suggests that US and European producers will have two increasingly viable options: (1) Perform the capital-intensive pre- and post-assembly tasks domestically while taking advantage of low wages in their peripheral zones for sewing. This would permit low production costs and a relatively quick turn around time; (2) Opt for integrated domestic garment production, counting on relatively rapid decline in the cost of robotic equipment and drastic time savings to compensate for any initial direct cost disadvantage.

While questions of automation and relative cost are undeniably important for projecting the future of world garment/textile competition, it would be a mistake to ignore the emerging strategic environment as well. We have earlier taken note of the current re-structuring of the US textile and garment industries, with movement toward more concentration. Both industries remain major employers in the US, and they have been sufficiently wounded by East Asian competition that the companies and labor unions are altering their historically antagonistic relationship in favor of cooperation for supporting technology research and building political influence.

While the prospect for cooperation *within* each industry seems favorable, there is an important element of natural antagonism between them. Garment producers are in favor of high tariffs on garments, but they have no reason to favor tariffs on the fabrics which are the raw material of their industry. Textile manufacturers, of course, do not have the same perspective. For the future of garment and textile exports from the NICs and new low-wage market entrants, much may depend on shifts in the balance of political power between these two industries in the US. If the US ends up with protection in garments and free trade in textiles, producers in the NICs will be at a double disadvantage. Our results suggest that Korean textile exports to the US are not cost-competitive with potential Chinese exports in the absence of quotas. At the same time, as Table 2.5 illustrates, protected US garment producers with access to non-taxed Chinese fabrics would enjoy a substantial cost advantage over Korean garment producers. Thus, a shift to duty-free imports of US fabrics could hurt Korean textile producers in two ways: By reducing their direct export market to the US, and by reducing the demand for their product by Korean garment producers.

Certainly, the patterns of international change will continue to be conditioned by the existing system of "managed" international trade. Export quotas have been set by historical benchmarks, and this currently limits the penetration of Chinese products in the US market. Similarly, the continued tariffs provide protection to the domestic industry from all Far Eastern competition. The situation is, therefore, evenly balanced at this point in time. Superior availability of automated capital goods and continued protection could lead to relatively rapid adoption of new technologies; on the other hand, cheap labor in China, other low-wage developing countries, and the OECD peripheral states could put a significant damper on technical change.

Whatever happens, it seems that the success stories of the past two decades – Korea, Taiwan and Hong Kong – will be severely challenged in the coming years. The textile and clothing industries are still of great importance to their economies, but our research indicates that both are increasingly ill-suited for the NICs' present circumstances. To state the major problem in the simplest possible way: in textiles and garments, the emerging race seems to be between microelectronics and very low-wage labor in China, the Caribbean, and elsewhere. Without protection, automation is currently too costly to prevent the low-wage workers from winning. The new microelectronics technology does offer savings in labor and time related costs, but these currently seem sufficient for dominance only in garment pre-assembly activities. In garment assembly and post-assembly, by contrast, sites in countries like China seem to retain a substantial cost advantage.

Thus, in the US market, Korea, Taiwan and Hong Kong should lose ground to both China and US/Caribbean joint operations in the next decade. This is consistent with the industry view that producers like China are in a position to swamp most markets if quotas are lifted. The NICs continue to have a cost advantage vis-a-vis stand-alone US production, though the gap has been narrowing.

While China and other low-wage states are formidable competitors at present, they will have to face difficult questions soon if they are to remain competitive into the next century. By all reasonable expectations, technology will move along, at a slower or faster pace depending on the exogenous flow of innovations and the industry response to their availability. The low-wage states will then be required to make technological transitions of their own. To the extent that current relatively labor intensive methods are very different from the newer technologies and those to come, this transaction could be painful unless the required human and physical capital is gradually brought together.

APPENDIX 2: TECHNOLOGY AND INPUT COST DATA FOR TEXTILE AND GARMENT PRODUCTION

TABLE A.2.1 *Synthetic-based fabric production: standard technologies*

		Spinning	
	Manual	Semi-Automatic	Robotic
Capacity per day (kg.)	5520	5520	5520
Initial load factor	90	92	94
Operators	100	14	2
Technicians	1	1	1
Engineers	0	0	1
Overhead workers	10	2	1
Materials ($)	.13	.13	.13
Eqpt. ($ million)	1.4	3.2	4
Bldg. size (sq.ft)	50000	30000	20000
Std. learn. time (years)	4	2	1
Final load factor	92	94	96

		Preparation	
	Manual	Semi-Automatic	Robotic
Capacity per day (yds)	60000	60000	60000
Initial load factor	94	95	96
Operators	127	31	8
Technicians	1	2	1
Engineers	0	1	2
Overhead workers	11	9	2
Materials ($)	.02	.02	.02
Eqpt. ($ million)	0.5	3	4.5
Bldg. size (sq.ft)	24000	20000	17000
Std. learn. time (years)	3	2	1
Final load factor	95	97	99

		Weaving	
	Manual	Semi-Automatic	Robotic
Capacity per day (yds)	60000	60000	60000
Initial load factor	98	98	98
Operators	300	44	12
Technicians	1	6	3
Engineers	0	1	3
Overhead workers	14	11	3
Materials ($)	.04	.04	.04
Eqpt. ($ million)	0.85	9	12
Bldg. Size (sq.ft)	40000	36000	23000
Std. learn time (years)	2	2	1
Final load factor	99	99	99

TABLE A.2.2 *Men's slacks: Standard technologies*

| | | Pre-Assembly | |
	Manual	Semi-Automatic	Robotic
Capacity per day	12000	12000	12000
Initial load factor	85	75	55
Operators	18	9	4
Technicians	4	4	4
Engineers	0	1	1
Overhead workers	1	1	1
Materials ($)	2.92	2.92	2.92
Eqpt. ($ million)	.0011	0.2241	0.3111
Bldg. size (sq.ft)	4420	10150	8120
Std. learn. time (years)	5	3	2
Time in process (days)	12	8	4
Final load factor	95	96	98

| | | Assembly | |
	Manual	Semi-Automatic	Robotic
Capacity per day	1200	1200	1200
Initial load factor	85	85	55
Operators	88	45	18
Technicians	1	1	1
Engineers	0	1	1
Overhead workers	4	2	1
Materials ($)	0.19	0.19	0.19
Eqpt. ($ million)	0.0506	0.1249	0.9
Bldg. size (sq.ft)	3900	4440	3550
Std. learn. time (years)	3	2	2
Time in process (days)	25	20	5
Final load factor	95	97	99

| | | Post-Assembly | |
	Manual	Semi-Automatic	Robotic
Capacity per day	1200	1200	1200
Initial load factor	95	93	90
Operators	16	8	4
Technicians	1	1	1
Engineers	0	1	1
Overhead workers	1	1	1
Materials ($)	0.08	0.08	0.08
Eqpt. ($ million)	.0091	0.0221	0.06
Bldg. size (sq.ft)	1010	880	700
Std. learn time (years)	2	2	1
Time in process (days)	5	4	1
Final load factor	99	99	99

TABLE A.2.3 *Men's single-needle long sleeve dress shirt: Standard technologies*

| | | Pre-Assembly | |
	Manual	Semi-Automatic	Robotic
Capacity per day	12000	12000	12000
Initial load factor	85	75	55
Operators	17	10	4
Technicians	4	4	4
Engineers	0	1	1
Overhead workers	1	1	1
Materials ($)	3.01	3.01	3.01
Eqpt. ($ million)	.0036	0.1551	0.215
Bldg. size (sq.ft)	3480	10410	8330
Std. learn. time (years)	5	3	2
Time in process (days)	12	8	4
Final load factor	95	96	98

| | | Assembly | |
	Manual	Semi-Automatic	Robotic
Capacity per day	1200	1200	1200
Initial load factor	85	85	55
Operators	71	32	12
Technicians	1	1	1
Engineers	0	1	1
Overhead workers	3	2	1
Materials ($)	0.14	0.14	0.14
Eqpt. ($ million)	0.066	0.1382	0.6
Bldg. size (sq.ft)	2500	5480	4380
Std. learn. time (years)	3	2	2
Time in process (days)	25	20	5
Final load factor	95	97	99

| | | Post-Assembly | |
	Manual	Semi-Automatic	Robotic
Capacity per day	1200	1200	1200
Initial load factor	95	93	90
Operators	13	6	3
Technicians	1	1	1
Engineers	0	1	1
Overhead workers	1	1	1
Materials ($)	0.22	0.22	0.22
Eqpt. ($ million)	0.0109	0.0163	0.045
Bldg. size (sq.ft)	640	1020	820
Std. learn time (years)	2	2	1
Time in process (days)	5	4	1
Final load factor	99	99	99

TABLE A.2.4   *Men's high style pullover shirt: standard technologies*

	Pre-Assembly		
	Manual	*Semi-Automatic*	*Robotic*
Capacity per day	12000	12000	12000
Initial load factor	85	75	55
Operators	18	10	4
Technicians	4	4	4
Engineers	0	1	1
Overhead workers	1	1	1
Materials ($)	1.26	1.26	1.26
Eqpt. ($ million)	.0074	0.2138	0.2975
Bldg. size (sq.ft)	4120	10650	8520
Std. learn. time (years)	5	3	2
Time in process (days)	12	8	4
Final load factor	95	96	98

	Assembly		
	Manual	*Semi-Automatic*	*Robotic*
Capacity per day	1200	1200	1200
Initial load factor	85	85	55
Operators	41	20	8
Technicians	1	1	1
Engineers	0	1	1
Overhead workers	2	1	1
Materials ($)	0.09	0.09	0.09
Eqpt. ($ million)	0.023	0.0278	0.4
Bldg. size (sq.ft)	1020	2210	1770
Std. learn. time (years)	3	2	2
Time in process (days)	25	20	5
Final load factor	95	97	99

	Post-Assembly		
	Manual	*Semi-Automatic*	*Robotic*
Capacity per day	1200	1200	1200
Initial load factor	95	93	90
Operators	8	4	2
Technicians	1	1	1
Engineers	0	1	1
Overhead workers	1	1	1
Materials ($)	0.17	0.17	0.17
Eqpt. ($ million)	.0038	0.0117	0.03
Bldg. size (sq.ft)	310	390	320
Std. learn time (years)	2	2	1
Time in process (days)	5	4	1
Final load factor	99	99	99

TABLE A.2.5 *Women's high style printed polyester dress: standard technologies*

| | | Pre-Assembly | |
	Manual	Semi-Automatic	Robotic
Capacity per day	12000	12000	12000
Initial load factor	85	75	55
Operators	19	10	4
Technicians	4	4	4
Engineers	0	1	1
Overhead workers	1	1	1
Materials ($)	6.22	6.22	6.22
Eqpt. ($ million)	.0025	0.2416	0.3398
Bldg. size (sq.ft)	4730	10010	8010
Std. learn. time (years)	5	3	2
Time in process (days)	12	8	4
Final load factor	95	96	98

| | | Assembly | |
	Manual	Semi-Automatic	Robotic
Capacity per day	1200	1200	1200
Initial load factor	85	85	55
Operators	65	35	14
Technicians	1	1	1
Engineers	0	1	1
Overhead workers	4	2	1
Materials ($)	0.15	0.15	0.15
Eqpt. ($ million)	0.0651	0.0711	0.7
Bldg. size (sq.ft)	2750	3040	2430
Std. learn. time (years)	3	2	2
Time in process (days)	25	20	5
Final load factor	95	97	99

| | | Post-Assembly | |
	Manual	Semi-Automatic	Robotic
Capacity per day	1200	1200	1200
Initial load factor	95	93	90
Operators	12	7	4
Technicians	1	1	1
Engineers	0	1	1
Overhead workers	1	1	1
Materials ($)	0.07	0.07	0.07
Eqpt. ($ million)	0.0107	0.0194	0.06
Bldg. size (sq.ft)	760	660	530
Std. learn time (years)	2	2	1
Time in process (days)	5	4	1
Final load factor	99	99	99

TABLE A.2.6 *Women's high style printed skirt: standard technologies*

| | | Pre-Assembly | |
	Manual	Semi-Automatic	Robotic
Capacity per day	12000	12000	12000
Initial load factor	85	75	55
Operators	19	10	4
Technicians	4	4	4
Engineers	0	1	1
Overhead workers	1	1	1
Materials ($)	3.88	3.88	3.88
Eqpt. ($ million)	.0025	0.2416	0.3398
Bldg. size (sq.ft)	4730	10010	8010
Std. learn. time (years)	5	3	2
Time in process (days)	12	8	4
Final load factor	95	96	98

| | | Assembly | |
	Manual	Semi-Automatic	Robotic
Capacity per day	1200	1200	1200
Initial load factor	85	85	55
Operators	41	17	6
Technicians	1	1	1
Engineers	0	1	1
Overhead workers	3	1	1
Materials ($)	0.08	0.08	0.08
Eqpt. ($ million)	0.0402	0.0333	0.3
Bldg. size (sq.ft)	1730	1480	1180
Std. learn. time (years)	3	2	2
Time in process (days)	25	20	5
Final load factor	95	97	99

| | | Post-Assembly | |
	Manual	Semi-Automatic	Robotic
Capacity per day	1200	1200	1200
Initial load factor	95	93	90
Operators	8	3	1
Technicians	1	1	1
Engineers	0	1	1
Overhead workers	1	1	1
Materials ($)	0.05	0.05	0.05
Eqpt. ($ million)	.0066	0.0091	0.015
Bldg. size (sq.ft)	0550	390	310
Std. learn time (years)	2	2	1
Time in process (days)	5	4	1
Final load factor	99	99	99

TABLE A.2.7 *Women's low style knit pullover shirt: standard technologies*

| | | Pre-Assembly | |
	Manual	Semi-Automatic	Robotic
Capacity per day	12000	12000	12000
Initial load factor	85	75	55
Operators	18	10	4
Technicians	4	4	4
Engineers	0	1	1
Overhead workers	1	1	1
Materials ($)	1.37	1.37	1.37
Eqpt. ($ million)	.0074	0.2138	0.2975
Bldg. size (sq.ft)	4120	10650	8520
Std. learn. time (years)	5	3	2
Time in process (days)	12	8	4
Final load factor	95	96	98

| | | Assembly | |
	Manual	Semi-Automatic	Robotic
Capacity per day	1200	1200	1200
Initial load factor	85	85	55
Operators	34	19	7
Technicians	1	1	1
Engineers	0	1	1
Overhead workers	2	1	1
Materials ($)	0.09	0.09	0.09
Eqpt. ($ million)	0.0187	0.0269	0.35
Bldg. size (sq.ft)	840	2150	1720
Std. learn. time (years)	3	2	2
Time in process (days)	25	20	5
Final load factor	95	97	99

| | | Post-Assembly | |
	Manual	Semi-Automatic	Robotic
Capacity per day	1200	1200	1200
Initial load factor	95	93	90
Operators	7	4	2
Technicians	1	1	1
Engineers	0	1	1
Overhead workers	1	1	1
Materials ($)	0.06	0.06	0.06
Eqpt. ($ million)	.0031	0.0113	0.03
Bldg. size (sq.ft)	270	380	310
Std. learn time (years)	2	2	1
Time in process (days)	5	4	1
Final load factor	99	99	99

TABLE A.2.8   *Input data*

	Korea	US	Jamaica	China
Daily wage for operators ($)	10	56	8	3
Daily wage for technicians ($)	25	88	15	6
Daily wage for engineers ($)	30	136	25	8
Daily wage for overhead workers ($)	15	104	15	6
Working days per year	300	250	250	250
Working hours per day	9	8	8	8
Bldg. constr. price ($/sq.ft.)	6	12	8	4
Interest rate (%)	10	8	10	15
Years for depreciating eqt.	5	5	5	5
Years for depreciating bldgs.	20	20	20	20

3 The NIC Challenge in Advanced Electronics

We concluded in the previous chapter that garments and textiles are showing signs of "de-maturing" with the advent of microelectronics-based production, data-processing, and communications systems. It seems likely that the higher wage NIC producers will experience a squeeze as competition increasingly centers on the race between cheap robots in the West and low-wage workers in poorer nations. The more successful producers may, of course, respond by following the OECD firms into more capital- and knowledge-intensive production. Given the relative scarcity of these factors in the NICs, however, the question of appropriate focus remains open.

In this chapter, we will examine the prospects of the NICs in technology intensive production by analyzing the state of competition near the technology frontier.[1] We will begin with a discussion of the general issues in electronics production. However, electronics products are quite varied. We will therefore use advanced semiconductor memories as the basis for our empirical analysis. We will attempt to place the emerging competition in memories in the more general context of high-technology electronics competition.

The primary assets of the industrial nations in the competitive struggle are, as always, their relative depth in technology, capital and human resources. Among the NICs which may mount a major challenge to the West in electronics are Brazil, South Korea, Taiwan, India and Singapore. These countries all have a relatively developed industrial base, a large stock of educated manpower, a commitment to R&D and a national policy of promoting the electronics industry. To summarize, we can say that they are operating in an environment that has both favorable and unfavorable aspects.

One of the favorable factors is the intensified international competition prompted by the process of technological convergence among electronics firms in the OECD countries. In seeking markets, these firms have been willing to transfer technology to, and from, alliances with firms in the NICs. In addition, increased competition has motivated firms (particularly US firms) to seek low cost production sites. This plant construction by multinational corporations (MNCs) has not always been beneficial to the NICs, but in some instances it has provided exposure to new technologies and trained local workers.

On the other hand, electronics industries have had high barriers to entry: the physical and human investment requirements have often been large and most evidence indicates that these requirements are increasing. The fierceness of international competition, which leads to greater availability of technology, also creates the need to learn quickly and price aggressively. Even firms in developed countries have often been unable to cope with these pressures and have sought government support in various ways.

The efforts made by NIC firms to date in international electronics are beginning to add up. Exports from newly industrializing countries are small relative to the three major exporters, Japan, United States and Germany. However, Korea, Taiwan and Singapore are approaching or have exceeded the levels of most other European countries. Their relative success to date contrasts strongly with that of much larger countries like Brazil and India. We shall give a brief account of some apparent reasons for the noticeable performance differences of the NICs. To anticipate, we conclude that Korea has followed both the most aggressive and the most coherent strategy. We will thus describe the nature of technological progress, learning and price competition in the semiconductor industry; and use our model of semiconductor costs to study the choice of technology in DRAM (dynamic random access memory) manufacture and examine the parameters affecting Korean prospects in this industry. We shall also use our model to comment on the alleged "dumping" of semiconductor memories by the Japanese. On Korea, our evidence suggests that the relatively narrow sales windows; the relative inexperience of Korean firms compared to US and Japanese firms; and the continuing need to make large investments puts Korea at a significant disadvantage. However, by taking the calculated risk and making itself a player in this market, Korea stands a better possibility than others of exploiting unexpected "opportunities", such as the US/Japan semiconductor pact and the appreciation of the Yen: both factors have had the effect of raising semiconductor prices.

NIC STRATEGIES IN ELECTRONICS

The first element of strategy we consider is the sequencing of products. This is followed by a consideration of the nature of scale economies, the size of the accessible market and the implication for cost reducing possibilities and behavior. Finally, we describe the major elements of government intervention to promote electronics industries in the NICs.

Product Choice and Sequencing

The main thrust in NICs has been towards manufacturing capability. The approaches followed have, however, been quite different. Electronics production in Taiwan and Korea was initiated in the late 1950s by Japanese and US firms seeking sites for low-cost production of components. The bulk of these components embodied elementary technology. Domestic entrepreneurs were soon attracted to this activity and a large number of small firms sprouted up. Even today this is a major sector in both the Korean and Taiwanese electronics industries. The component firms were unable to grow or diversify into other products and hence have continued to be small. However, they have served at least two useful purposes. First, they stimulated the development of a capital goods industry which produced the machinery required for the assembly of components. Secondly, as the consumer electronics sector in these countries developed, there was a cost-competitive supply of components available. The ready availability of high quality and low cost components is continuing to provide Korean and Taiwanese producers a competitive edge as they are moving into office automation products.

The consumer electronics sector in Korea and Taiwan has been the main driver of growth. The Korean conglomerates, Goldstar and Samsung, and the larger of the Taiwanese firms, Tatung and Sampo, became involved in this sector in the late 1950s and 1960s. The product choice within the consumer sector was determined essentially by demand trends in the US. The choice was conditioned by the perceived degree of Japanese competition. The Japanese attempt has been to continuously differentiate their products and hence generate markets that are relatively price-inelastic; the Korean and Taiwanese response has been to follow into the price-elastic (mass) market left behind by the Japanese. In the 1980s, Korean and Taiwanese firms began an attempt to close the gap vis-à-vis the Japanese. They have sought to differentiate their designs and to enter markets for more advanced products.

Thus, the Koreans and Taiwanese followed a sequential approach to product selection for about two decades. By the early 1980s, they had a well developed component base; large firms with experience in consumer goods manufacturing and marketing; and a well developed manpower base. The Koreans, in particular, and the Taiwanese to a lesser extent are trying to use these advantages to increase their competitive strength in the high-technology sector. The current Korean and Taiwanese approach may be characterized as a big push, in as much as the firms and the two governments are engaged in promoting products and technologies across the technology spectrum.[2]

At the other extreme, India has had no sequencing strategy. For the last two decades, the division of production between components, consumer electronics, industrial electronics (including defense) and communications has remained roughly equal. As a consequence, one of India's major weaknesses is a very poorly developed component base. Furthermore, there are only weak institutional linkages between the different electronics sectors, making coordination extremely difficult. Brazil has similar problems. The institutional linkages are probably even weaker in Brazil. The consumer electronics sector has developed in isolation from the computer or "informatics" sector; and despite similarity in government policy, the communications and "informatics" sectors do not seem to have developed linkages.

Thus, India and Brazil have sought to develop all parts of the electronics complex, but without capturing technological linkages between the different sectors and without fostering institutional linkages which could have exploited the technical links. The different pattern of sequencing in Korea/Taiwan as against Brazil/India is related to differences in market orientation. Korea and Taiwan have been heavily dependent on exports whereas Brazil and India have produced essentially for their domestic markets. Korea and Taiwan have taken advantage of international trade, producing in large quantities a small set of products and importing what was not produced. Brazil and India have attempted to produce a wide range of products to satisfy domestic demand. The small size of the internal market in both countries has been compounded by uncertainties (including those stemming from the lack of direction in government policy); as such, there has been an incentive to diversify into new products rather than to expand in the same line of production.

Factors Influencing Cost Competitiveness

Cost competitiveness in the NICs has been influenced by a number of interrelated factors: product sequencing, choice of markets (export and domestic), institutional development, economies of scale achieved and the degree of competition. For a given market size, the achievement of economies of scale is impeded if there are too many product lines or if there are too many competitors for the same product line. The existence of too many product lines essentially impacts the development of the component sector. The Indian electronics industry, for example, has been caught in a trap of small scales of component output. Component prices have been high, resulting in a high price and low demand for final products. That in turn has meant a low volume of demand for components: hence the underdeveloped state of the component industry. On account of the poor market availability, many systems producers are forced to produce some required components in house. The small internal requirements result in loss of scale economies and spread the limited technical and managerial resources thinner over the activities of the firm. A similar problem can stem from too many firms. In Brazil, Frischtak (1986, p. 51) has suggested that "unrestricted entry of national firms in a market of limited economic size may have been responsible for the large unit costs of data processing equipment". According to his assessment, Brazilian data processing firms have been unable to achieve *technological* economies of scale.

Competition has also been high in Taiwan. Unlike the Brazilian case, where the competition has largely been among domestic firms in the mini/microcomputer industry, in Taiwan both foreign and domestic firms have competed. In Taiwan, because of the export orientation, at least a few large domestic firms have been able to set up plants that capture technological scale economies. What the Taiwanese firms have lacked, in comparison with Korean conglomerates, is *organizational* economies of scale. In the buying of inputs and (more so) in international marketing efforts, Korean firms have been able to do much better because they have sold large volumes of individual product lines. For a period of time, Taiwanese firms had larger exports of personal computer systems than their Korean counterparts. However, in the past two years, Daewoo and Hyundai have begun marketing very large volumes of personal computers. "The Koreans have poured $100 million into new computer plants to improve efficiency and have been quoting prices that the Taiwanese are struggling to match. To keep up, the Taiwanese have cut prices, but the Koreans can quickly outpace them by switching factories from TV and VCR production to computers if necessary."[3]

Korean producers have also been successful in more sophisticated markets. An example is a highly price competitive color graphics and publishing workstation designed and manufactured by Samsung Semiconductor and Telecommunications and distributed by MicroDirect.[4] Similarly, Korean firms have begun marketing a number of their products in the US under their own brand names; Taiwanese firms are a considerable way from reaching that stage.

The need for economies of scale conflicts with the need to maintain a competitive environment. An attempt can be made to balance these requirements, as for example, in the Brazilian telecommunications equipment industry, where four firms have been allowed to participate. It was believed that four firms would be sufficient to provide a high degree of competition without reducing the potential for achieving scale economies. However, it has been difficult to achieve either a significant amount of competition or cost reductions. Ericsson do Brazil controls about half of the Brazilian switching equipment market but produces at a cost 25 per cent greater than at its parent company in Sweden. At least part of the reason, as in India, is the high cost of components.

The only country that has been able to achieve the "right" balance is Korea. The Korean electronics consumer and industrial electronics industry has been very oligopolistic. Three firms (Samsung, Goldstar and Daewoo) have dominated the industry. The oligopolistic market structure has been accompanied by severe competition. The firms have competed, both in the domestic and export markets, through price, quality and marketing strategies. Also each company has chosen to produce entire product lines (for example, each firm typically produces an entire range of televisions rather than specializing in a few models); this makes competition even more intense. A number of fierce battles have been fought in the domestic market for video cassette recorders and personal computers.[5]

Thus, while the outlet provided by an export market helps, its lack of sufficiency is suggested by the example of Taiwan. Competitive ability in international markets requires large resources for marketing. Only the Korean firms have developed to the size necessary for being serious international competitors.

While much of the market growth registered has been in basic electronic products, this is far from having been universally the case.

Indeed, there is a real possibility that some NICs may leapfrog to the technology frontier in select areas. The most striking example of this possibility is seen in the Korean effort to produce dynamic random access memories.

Strategic Government Intervention

Despite theoretical critiques of strategic government intervention, the role of the government in industrial targeting has increased only in recent years. In this regard there has been little difference between developed and newly industrializing countries either in the range of policies used or in the resolve in implementation.[6] In the rest of this section, we describe government policies with regard to import protection, foreign investment and education/research.

Import protection

Protection of the domestic market from imports has been a major policy tool for most NICs. Market reserve has been practiced by Brazil, Korea and India in a significant manner. Singapore and Hong Kong are possibly the only two states that have had open economies. Korea has used import protection at successive stages to promote its domestic firms. During the phase when Korea was developing as a major consumer electronics producer, Korea did not permit the import of its major export: televisions. In the 1980s, Korea began to produce computers; the government selectively protected the domestic market against foreign competition. Since Korean producers are not yet capable of producing high-end computers, the government has protected the mini and micro computer markets. The government passed legislation to restrict imports of computers and peripherals into Korea in 1983. The law prohibited the import of most microcomputers and some minicomputers, as well as selected models of disk drives, printers, terminals and tape drives. Under the regulations, some exemptions are allowed for imported products destined for use in process control, R&D or other specialized applications. But exceptions are granted only in the most extenuating circumstances.

A similar position exists in the telecommunication sector. "The importation of almost all important telecommunication equipment is subject to case-by-case recommendation by the Electronic Industries Association of Korea... Before a license will be issued, this association must certify that any given import license application involves a product or products not currently manufacturered in Korea" (Kim, 1985, p. 6).

The only major sector with a low degree of import protection in Korea is semiconductors. There are two possible reasons for this. The initiative for production of advanced semiconductors came from domestic firms rather than from the government. In fact, the official view on these ventures was hostile at least until recently. Moreover, the firms obviously felt that they could manage without market protection. A large market exists within the conglomerates and so protection was less necessary than in the earlier cases. Further, the firms have developed the capacity to sustain losses over significant periods of time and so are less dependent on subsidization in the form of domestic market protection. Though this is an achievement, the Koreans may yet be in trouble with regard to the emerging international trade regime. The transfer of subsidization from government control to conglomerates with "deep pockets" is not viewed favourably by US trade administrators. If Korean semiconductor firms start gaining significant market shares, they could well come under scrutiny for "dumping".[7]

Despite Korea's potential problems with "dumping" issues, Korea is the only NIC which has made effective use of its import protection policies. Korean firms have used the period of protection to gain experience and move down the learning curve. They have also made effective use of the domestic market during periods when world demand for their products has been weak. In contrast, Brazil and India have had more stringent import protection policies but have been unable to produce internationally competitive products even after long periods of protection. Thus, while market protection can be a useful device for promoting domestic firms, it is clearly not a substitute for making hard choices with regard to products and institutions.

Foreign investment

Once again, the three countries that have followed the most restrictive policies are Brazil, India and Korea. Domestic producers are generally unable to compete with TNCs (transnational corporations). The TNCs have a number of advantages: better reputation, greater access to technology, and greater economies of scale in production, raising capital and marketing. Goverments seeking to foster domestic entrepreneurship are therefore inclined to put restrictions on TNCs. On the other hand, where the gap between domestic producers and TNC capabilities is very large, the costs of promoting domestic entrepreneurship can be high. There is thus a conflict involved in promoting domestic entrepreneurs; the manner in which the conflict plays out depends on the balance of forces within the country.

Two contrasting models are those of Brazil and Korea. Brazil has sought to create national capability in its computer and communications industries. The development of capability in the computer industry in the 1970s was promoted from within the state apparatus by technically trained bureaucrats. [8]

In the early 1970s, Brazil had a substantial stock of engineers and scientists who had been trained in its own universities; some of them had also done graduate work in the United States. They had a strong commitment to the creation of a domestic computer industry. In 1972, an interministerial commission under the Ministry of Planning was set up to regulate the computer industry. Known as CAPRE (Commission for the Coordination of Electronic Data Processing Activities), it became the main vehicle for the realization of domestic technical interests. In the mid-1970s, the focus was on preventing foreign competition in the minicomputer market. Production capabilities never quite reached international standards, but some degree of local learning took place. Domestic computer firms did more R&D and employed more engineers relative to sales than did the TNCs. In 1977, CAPRE was dissolved and SEI (Special Secretariat for Informatics) was set up to guide computer policy. SEI had new personnel with much less technical competence than the CAPRE engineers. However, the CAPRE policies were carried forward and even strengthened, with the emergence of a new focus of attention: the microcomputer.

Korea has also followed very restrictive policies vis-a-vis foreign investment. However, there have been important differences between Korea and Brazil. The crucial difference has been that major Korean industrial groups, unlike their Brazilian counterparts, have had an active interest in electronics; indeed, electronics has been in the vanguard of their efforts. To a large extent, therefore, technological nationalism and industrial capital have coalesced in the Korean conglomerates, creating a stronger basis for restriction of foreign investment.

In the 1980s Korean firms have been seeking greater access to foreign technology. To the extent possible they have tried to buy technology through licensing agreements. Where licensing has not been sufficient, they have entered into joint ventures. Most of these licensing agreements and joint ventures have been with US firms since Japanese firms have been very reluctant to share technology with the Koreans.[9] US firms have viewed an increased presence in Korea as an important marketing strategy. For example, Dr Robert N. Noyce, Intel's Vice-Chairman, rationalized his company's link with Samsung as follows:

We believe Samsung's experience in manufacturing and their commitment to this sector will help spread the presence of the Intel architecture in the Pacific Basin to our mutual advantage. (*Business Korea*, March 1985, p. 62).

The Korean conglomerates have been forming joint ventures with US firms from a much stronger position than most developing country or NIC firms have been able to secure; hence, the Koreans have been able to negotiate greatly superior technology transfer deals.[10]

Technology policy

Though general educational policies have been critical to forming a base of scientists and engineers, specialized institutions have been found necessary to gain faster access to information technologies. The performance of these institutions has depended on their scale of operation, their degree of commercial orientation and on the strengths and weaknesses of domestic firms.

Korea

The Korean Institute of Science and Technology (KAIST), the Korean Institute of Electronics Technology (KIET) and the Korea Telecommunications Research Institute (KETRI) have been the principal institutions focused on electronics-related technology. KAIST has been charged with the responsibility of producing the several thousand Ph.D.s and Masters degree holders that the Korean electronics industry needs. The commercial tasks of product and process development have largely been with KIET and KETRI – operating for the past couple of years as one unit, Electronics and Telecommunications Research Institute (ETRI). KIET was set up in 1979 to provide a demonstration that semiconductors could be produced in Korea. By the early 1980s, Korean conglomerates had outgrown KIET capabilities by licensing foreign technology and setting up internal R&D departments and "technology-watch" outposts in the Silicon Valley in California. For a period of time, Daewoo negotitated the purchase of KIET's semiconductor production facility, but eventually Goldstar bought that plant. Daewoo instead bought Zymos, a US firm, to gain access to semiconductor technology.

KIET proved to be a catalyst; however, it could not continue to function as a common semiconductor research center for domestic industry because of strong competition and mutual suspicion among the large Korean firms. ETRI has, like KIET, been primarily playing a vanguard role. It is, for example, engaged in developing: communications protocol for the Integrated Services Digital Network, optical transmission devices, and an earth-station for satellite communications.[11]

Taiwan

The Electronics Research and Service Organization (ERSO) is the focus of public research, and the Hshinchu Science City is a location promoted for gaining technological synergies in the manner of the Silicon Valley. ERSO has had a strong commercial focus: one of the two silicon foundries in Taiwan belongs to it. More new foundries are being built by private entrepreneurs. ERSO has had much closer ties with domestic industry than KIET in Korea. The Taiwanese firms are much smaller than the Korean firms and hence have a smaller capacity to undertake independent research initiatives. As such, the public role and the degree of cooperation between firms is high in Taiwan.

Brazil

Despite the importance accorded to the computer sector, no special institution was developed for doing research on computer technology. The research has been conducted mainly within the firms (and to some extent in university departments). Brazilian firms have had very high R&D to sales ratios (8 to 10 per cent) and they have also had a large proportion of engineers in their work-force. The absence of significant public research is probably explained by the fact that the mini and micro computer technologies were considered widely known.

An institution was created for telecommunications research. This Research and Development Center, referred to as CPqD, carries out its own research program and also coordinates research at universities and in the industry. The universities are supposed to do basic research; CPqD and the industry share the tasks of prototype and product development. Brazil has followed a big push policy in telecommunications. This has involved an across the board attempt at technological competence; there have been some successes and some failures. Electromechanical switching has been an example of successful technology development, whereas transmission systems have been more difficult to master. In the area of digital switching, the Brazilians have developed small exchanges but they have been unable to develop large digital systems.

India

India has a number of electronics research facilities. In addition, Indian electronics firms, like their Brazilian counterparts, have devoted large shares of their sales to R&D. Even more than in Brazil, however, the Indian research efforts have been dispersed and diffuse. The small scale of the efforts has entailed very low research productivity. Moreover, the public research institutions have had very little link with commercial (or market) requirements.

The Centre for Development of Telematics (CDOT) is an exception to the general characterization of the Indian R&D sector. CDOT is developing small digital exchanges. It has had a strong commercial orientation from the start. It has sought to design its products with a common set of components and to work with producers in order to make possible efficient component production. It is, however, early to judge whether this approach will be successful since production based on CDOT technology is yet to begin.

Singapore

The Singapore Government's efforts have been mainly focused on manpower development. For manufacturing technology, Singapore depends on the R&D efforts of multinationals. In keeping with its goal of being a major center of information technology, Singapore set up three computer training and research institutes in 1981 and 1982. These are the Institute of Systems Science (ISS), a partnership between IBM and the National University of Singapore; the Japan Singapore Institute of Software Technology, a joint research project between the Governments of Singapore and Japan; and the Center for Computer Studies, a partnership between ICL and Ngee Ann Polytechnic (Government of Singapore, 1985). The emphasis is on developing capability in artificial intelligence techniques, gaining expertise in software production under the UNIX operating environment, and increasing software productivity through the use of program generators and other software tools.

COMPETITIVE DYNAMICS IN SEMICONDUCTOR MEMORIES

In this section we shall empirically examine the evolution of costs of producing semiconductor memories, the pricing strategies adopted by major firms and recent market developments. All cost calculations in this section are based on the model of dynamic cost comparisons described in Appendix 3.

Movement of the Technology Frontier

The semiconductor industry has been characterized by a rapid rate of technological improvement. The industry is relatively new, and a considerable backlog of knowledge in physics, chemistry, electrical and mechanical engineering has been brought to bear. New disciplines of computer science and engineering have developed at the same time, and these have facilitated improvements in production. In addition, there has been a rapidly growing demand for semiconductors. The demand has increasingly shifted towards more sophisticated products, creating large incentives to upgrade the technology. Of course, the growth in demand has itself been a function of the lower prices made possible by technological evolution, so that technological change and increased demand have fed on each other.

To understand the nature of technological evolution in the semiconductor industry, we need first of all to define the concept. There are two senses in which we talk of technological improvement or progress. There is a sense of progress wherein the focus of attention is a purely physical achievement. For example, the production of ever smaller integrated circuits (chips) and the consequent miniaturization of electronics systems is often associated with technical progress. But miniaturization represents progress in a deeper sense than is reflected in the physical achievement. We can state unambiguously that the technology of production has improved when the same output is produced by fewer (or a lower level of) inputs. And indeed, miniaturization has involved just that.

While the physical progress has been impressive and is well documented, it is clearly the economics that have driven these capacity enhancements. Dynamic random access memories (DRAMs) are useful as examples, since these memories have served essentially the same purpose across several product generations. In addition, they are large volume commodity products constituting a major segment of the semiconductor market. The memory capacity of a DRAM has gone up by a factor of four with every transition from one generation to the next. Until the late 1970s, the "life" of each generation was around five years. However, the most recent generation, the 256K DRAM, was introduced in late 1985 and a number of firms began supplying the 1–M DRAM in sample quantities by mid-1987, indicating that the 256K chip would have a life of less than three years. [12]

When more elements are packed into a smaller space on the silicon wafer, there is a saving in the cost of silicon. However, increased density of elements also leads to greater error and hence lower yield (or productivity), thus increasing the costs. At the same time, capital costs also go up because superior equipment is needed to pack the electronic components into tinier areas of real estate. The force of miniaturization has thus far been stronger: Even though the number of good chips per wafer has fallen when "line-widths" have been reduced (particularly in the early phases of a new product generation) and even though capital costs have gone up progressively, the cost *per bit* of memory has fallen from one generation to the next because memory capacity has increased four-fold. It is in this sense, in the decline in cost per bit of memory, that we can say there has been technological evolution in semiconductor manufacturing.

Though the cost per byte of memory has been going down, the absolute costs have all been going up. The importance of absolute costs arises quite simply because capital markets are not perfect. There are capital limitations, both at the level of a country and at the level of a firm. It is also necessary to note that the upfront capital costs do not adequately reflect capital requirements in the semiconductor industry. Working capital needs also go up tremendously as the movement from one generation to another occurs. Both the labor and materials supply costs have increased rapidly in the past. Indeed, it is interesting to note that in moving from the 4K to the 64K generation, the fixed capital/labor ratio went down: the cost of labor grew faster than that of capital. Clearly, the composition of labor changes is important and the simple capital/labor ratio does not tell the whole story. In interviews with industry experts, it was emphasized that the importance of engineers and technicians has increased considerably over successive product generations. Given the close attention that is required in controlling the production process, such a shift in the composition of the labor force is not really surprising. Up to the 64K generation, human skill played a particularly important role in reducing costs. However, the rise in capital costs for the 256K chip has been much greater than the rise in labor cost and it is clear that productivity increase is going to be embodied more and more in the capital goods themselves. Of course, this does not mean that human skills will cease to be important. In the manufacturing process itself, and more so in the design of machines and processes, human skill will continue to be a critical input.

The Role of Learning

In the previous subsection we discussed the implications of technological evolution in semiconductor manufacturing. The main emphasis was on progress embodied in superior capital goods, which make it possible to reduce the line-width and to handle larger silicon wafers. Such progress is strictly available only to all who can purchase the capital goods: several major vendors of capital equipment exist, and the market seems to be quite competitive.

There is, however, the technical progress that occurs after the equipment is installed. It is described in the business and economics literature in the form of learning, experience or progress functions. The semiconductor industry is not only quite special in the speed of movement of its technology frontier, but it also has a very pronounced learning curve. The costs of producing a new generation of product typically fall sharply and the speed of such a decline determines the profits and hence the competitive dynamics.

The manufacture of semiconductors proceeds in three stages: wafer fabrication, assembly and testing.[13] In the first stage a wafer is processed such that several chips (or dies) are outlined on the wafer. Each chip is the eventual semiconductor device. At the next stage the dies are sawed off the wafer and packaged (or assembled). The assembled chips are finally tested.

The learning process involves producing a larger number of good dies from a given wafer. In industry language, this is referred to as improving the yield. The factors that lead to yield improvement at the wafer processing stage are as follows: (1) reduction of defects on the wafer; (2) improving the compatibility of the various devices on a particular chip; and (3) improving the chip design.

The first two factors are dependent on processing improvements. Such improvements are achieved through trial and error by manufacturing engineers, technicians, and operators. The improvements in design are usually achieved by engineers who are not involved on a regular basis in the manufacturing process, though obviously they must have some interaction with the shop-floor engineers and technicians. At the assembly stage, the learning process involves greater operator efficiency in manual operations as well as in machine handling. Clearly, therefore, the learning process is hastened if the work force has superior training and diligence. This also means that learning can be diffused across firms through the movement of people. Learning may be partially embodied in improved machinery. But according to industry experts, the learning process has to be gone through even with improved machinery. Software which may control processes very finely and hence obviate the need for learning as described above has yet to be developed.

Learning has been described above as a deterministic process. However, there is considerable uncertainty in the relationship between inputs and outputs at each stage of the learning curve. Even within plants in a given firm and indeed within the same plant, the output has been observed to vary for completely unknown reasons. For instance, the clean room may get contaminated and no one may know the source or extent of this contamination. Some firms attain better yields than others by devising "tricks" in the wafer processing stage; tricks are often traded. However, there is some degree of randomness in arriving at such tricks.

Michael Spence (1981) has argued that reduction of costs via learning will have its most significant impact when the speed of learning is neither too fast nor too slow. When learning rates are either very fast or very slow, the cost differentials between industry leaders and followers will be relatively small and hence the industry will be fairly competitive. When learning rates are in the intermediate range, cost differentials among firms will be significant and significant barriers to entry will exist.

Available information is not easy to interpret since most learning curve estimates are based on price declines. Hence, issues relating to industry structure and pricing mechanisms become important in analyzing learning curve estimates. The available evidence does, however, suggest that learning in the semiconductor industry has been rapid relative to other industries. A recent study (Ghemawat, 1985) compiled learning curve estimates for 97 products and found that on average a doubling of the output was associated with a 15 per cent cost reduction. As against that, costs in the semiconductor industry have fallen by 30 per cent with doubling of output. In addition, since the semiconductor market has been growing very rapidly, the time interval over which output has doubled has been shorter than in other industries and hence significant cost reductions have taken place over shorter time spans than in almost any other major industrial sector.

The possibility of relatively rapid learning rates and fast growth of demand have reduced somewhat the disadvantage of late entry into the semiconductor market. However, it is extremely important to note that this observation does not by itself suggest that new entrants have a guarantee of success. The main caveat is that learning speeds mean very little by themselves. They must been seen in relation to the planning horizon. In the case of the semiconductor industry, new products have displaced old products at fairly short intervals. Earlier we discussed technological evolution in the DRAM market and pointed out that the cost per bit of memory has been falling with every successive generation. Hence, whenever a new generation has become viable, the demand for the previous generation product has fallen off sharply. Each product has therefore had an economic life of less than five years. The large profits have been made in the first few years (as we shall discuss in some detail below), and so latecomers have been at a significant disadvantage. In addition, the evidence suggests considerable dispersion in learning rates within the semiconductor industry. One dimension of this dispersion is international: among industry experts, a common perception is that Japanese learning rates have been more rapid than the US rates. That raises the question whether either the US or the Japanese learning rates can be replicated in a third country. These issues are discussed below in considerable quantitative detail.

Price-cost Margins across the Learning Curve

The prices of most semiconductor products shows a sharp decline over a period of 4–5 years. However, on the basis of interviews with industry experts we infer that the cost declines are even sharper.

According to the best information available to us, costs fall relatively rapidly over the first two years of ramped-up production and then fall more slowly, nearing the lower limit by about the end of the third year. Since the cost decline is sharper than the price decline, the first market entrants derive considerable rents from high price-cost margins. This factor has had significant influence on the nature of competition in the semiconductor industry.

The accompanying graphs compare the average market prices and factory production costs for successive generations of DRAMs.[14] In interpreting these data, it should be borne in mind that the cost decline considered is along an industry average learning curve and that US learning conditions are assumed. The following story emerges:

1. For the three generations of products considered, the price-cost ratio has risen rapidly as production has begun to ramp up. For a number of quarters, the margin has remained relatively high; it is presumably during this period that the large profits have been made; the ratio has then fallen as competition has increased and as the new product generation has begun to appear viable (see Figures 3.1, 3.2 and 3.3.). Though this general picture holds for all three DRAM types, there have been significant intergenerational differences.

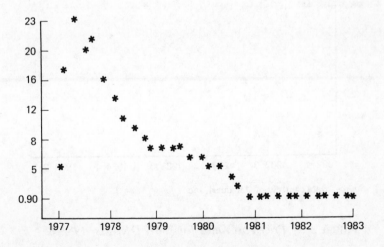

FIGURE 3.1   *Price/cost ratios for 16K DRAMs, 1977–83*

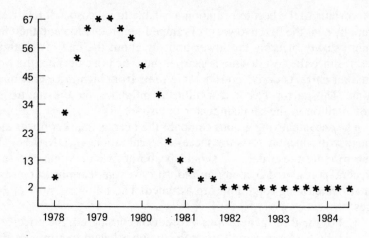

Source: Data courtesy of Dataquest, Inc.

FIGURE 3.2   *Price/cost ratios for 64K DRAMs, 1978–85*

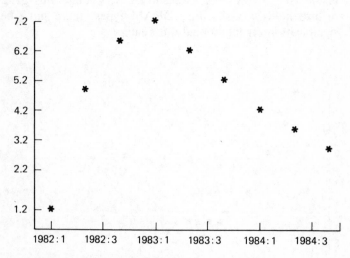

Source: Data courtesy of Dataquest, Inc.

FIGURE 3.3   *Price/cost ratios for 256K DRAMs, 1982–85*

2. The price-cost ratio rose the most for the 64K DRAM and least for the most recent product, the 256K DRAM.

3. According to industry experts, a firm breaks even when the price/factory cost ratio is about 2. In other words, an amount which is roughly equal to the factory cost at its asymptotic level is needed to cover administrative, marketing and other miscellaneous expenses. It should then be noted that for the 16K DRAM, the ratio remained in the region of 4 for about 6 quarters. In the case of the 64K and 256K DRAMs, the fall to the ratio of 2 has been much quicker.

4. The economic life of successive generations has become successively shorter. In the case of 16K chips, profits were made for about 5 years; however, the life of the 64K chip was about 4 years and that of the 256K chip may be less than 3 years.

5. Thus, significant profits were made in the 16K and in the early phase of the 64K generations. The huge price-cost margin in the early phase of the 64K generation suggests that there was a relatively inelastic demand for the product during that period. In the late 1970s, therefore, the profit margins clearly appeared attractive and this was bound to attract new firms.

6. In the 64K DRAM market, the Japanese firms took advantage of the large gaps between price and costs and gained large market shares through aggressive pricing. After an initial steady decline, the price of the 64K chip went through a period of relatively rapid fall. The latter period was the phase during which the Japanese increased and consolidated their market share. On average, the Japanese had about a third of the 16K market, about two-thirds of the 64K market and seem to have almost all the 256K market.

7. In order to confirm the robustness of the analysis above, we have recalculated the price-cost margins for the 64K chip under a set of assumptions somewhat different from those which form the basis for Figure 3.2. In Figure 3.2, we assumed that the cost decline started in the first quarter of 1978 when the first shipments of the 64K chip were made. However, the quantity of shipments was very small in 1978. The price-cost ratio was reestimated on the assumption that the learning process really began in 1979 when significant quantities began to be shipped. Although the early sample quantities were shipped mainly by the Japanese, major American firms (Motorola, Texas Instruments) entered soon after and captured more than half of the

market. At this point (first quarter of 1980), the price-cost ratio was about 40. The Japanese producers then took a series of price initiatives, lowering the price-cost margin but capturing a larger share of the market.

One final point needs to be added to this story. The Japanese at all points had somewhat higher margins than the American producers. The extent of this advantage was historically not very large; it is, however, believed that greater automation may have increased the advantage in recent years. None of this contradicts the basic idea developed above that the large profits in the 16K and 64K markets attracted a number of Japanese firms, which captured the DRAM markets by price cutting, reducing the margins available to all firms including themselves.

Recent Developments

During the past few years, the semiconductor memory business may have set a new standard for turbulence. The demand for semiconductor memories fell by about 25 per cent from $3.5 billion in 1984 to $2.6 billion in 1985. The spectacular successes of 1984 had induced very heavy capital investment. The prospects seemed good even to Korean conglomerates, which announced investments of over $1 billion. The sharp fall in demand in the face of growing production capacity led to dramatic price declines, even by the standards of the semiconductor industry. The price of the 64K dynamic random access memory (DRAM) was around $3.00 in 1984; towards the end of 1985, it was selling at about 50 cents. The price of the 256K DRAM fell from $32 in the first quarter of 1984 to $16.50 in the last quarter; by the end of 1985, the 256K DRAM was selling at around $2.00.

Nineteen eighty-five was critical also because the 256K/64K price ratio fell to about 4, creating the economic basis for a shift away from the 64K DRAM to the 256K DRAM. While the Japanese share of the 64K market in 1984 was only 58 per cent, their share in the 256K market was about 92 per cent. The Japanese thus had a head start over the US firms in the production of 256K DRAMs. This earlier start, as we shall discuss below, translated into a cost advantage and helped the Japanese in maintaining their market share. All major US producers except Texas Instruments have left the 256K market. Among the smaller producers, Micron Technology continues to maintain that it is still a player for the 256K round.

Several major US electronics firms apparently decided to respond to the Japanese challenge by joining the protectionist chorus. Micron Technology filed dumping charges against several Japanese producers of 64K chips. Intel, National Semiconductor and AMD filed dumping charges against Japaneses producers of erasable programmable read-only memory (EPROM) chips. The US government seems to have gotten the message:

> The U.S. Commerce Department handed down a preliminary ruling on 64K dumping which supported Micron Technology. Final rulings by the Commerce Department and the U.S. International Trade Commission (ITC) further endorsed the dumping charge.

> More significantly, the U.S. Department of Commerce (at the instigation of a cabinet-level Trade Policy Group) filed its own dumping charges against Japanese 256K DRAM producers (and, in an interesting new twist, flirted with the idea of "prospective" dumping charges against 1M producers, even before they had shipped the chips!).[15]

Japanese firms were not slow to read the handwriting on the wall: Nippon Electric Company (NEC) and other Japanese majors have since announced hefty price increases. For US producers, this should provide a temporary reprieve. However, consumers have immediately rechristened the Japanese as "greedy monopolists". Under the circumstances, they might be forgiven for concluding that they can have it neither way.

In spite of everything, the race for future DRAM markets is already on. Several US and Japanese firms are now shipping 1M (megabyte) DRAMS. For industry-watchers and high-technology buffs, this is all endlessly entertaining, of course. We also think that it raises some important analytical issues which must be sorted out before effective strategies for high technology competition can be identified. Two issues seem particularly important. Firstly, what forces have driven intertemporal pricing policies in the semiconductor industry? Secondly, have Japanese firms in fact been "dumping" memory chips? An understanding of these issues necessarily requires an analysis of the industry in terms of learning speeds, entry timing, and firm strategies with regard to pricing and the adoption of new technologies.

OPTIMUM TECHNOLOGY CHOICE AND DYNAMIC COST
COMPETITION

This section will report on a set of simulation experiments which
address many of the questions which have been discussed in the
preceding sections. The simulations are generated by our dynamic
costing model, which is described in the Appendix to this chapter.
We shall first consider 64K DRAM production. To provide useful
contrast, the simulations employ data from three economies at very
different levels of income per capita: Korea, the US and India. India
is included because it clearly has the scientific/technical resources and
skills to become a player in electronics if it can solve a host of
infrastructure and policy problems. Indian labor at all skill levels is
far cheaper than Korea's. Thus, evaluating the technologies at Indian
wage rates allows us to determine the boundaries of technological
choice. We shall also consider 256K DRAM production and compare
the prospects of the US, Japan and Korea.

   We focus here on Korea because, as indicated in the discussion
above, Korea is in the best position to move to the technology
frontier and indeed has made significant investments in that direction. Several major Korean firms have decided that semiconductor
production will be a major element in their new emphasis on direct
competition in high-technology sectors with US and Japanese producers. Recent announcements suggest that significant investments in
plant and equipment have been made and more are in the offing. The
Korean firms' plan apparently rests on three foundations: (1)
Substantial investment in facilities for design, product development,
and testing in California's Silicon Valley; (2) construction of facilities
in Korea to mass produce DRAMS for export; and (3) targeted
support by the Korean government.

Investments in the United States

Four Korean conglomerates have set up subsidiaries in the Silicon
Valley (though one has largely withdrawn). It is clear that a unique
hybrid stategy is being employed: the facilities are located in the US
and employ graduates of US scientific and technical institutions:
however, many of these graduates are in fact Korean nationals. In
pursuing this policy, the Korean enterprises seem to be attempting to
maximize loyalty and discretion among their employees while bowing
to the apparent preference of many for remaining in the US.

The first Korean firm to achieve start-up in the US was Tristar, a subsidiary of Samsung. Tristar began by producing 64K DRAMS with 5-inch wafers, using a technology purchased from a US firm, Micron Technology. Tristar's production target for 1984 was 2 million 64K DRAMs, and it has announced plans to begin production of 256K DRAMs sometime in 1985. Samsung itself has announced plans to market 1M DRAMs at an indeterminate point in the future.

Goldstar has invested $60 million in a design center in Sunnyvale, California. This center has the capacity to perform custom design services for US clients. In addition, it serves as the agent for purchasing advanced equipment for Goldstar's manufacturing facilities in Korea. In Silicon Valley, there are persistent rumors to the effect that Goldstar has been negotiating with AMD and other local firms to provide them financial support in exchange for access to advanced VLSI technology.

Hyundai, which is entering this arena for the first time, established Modern Electrosystems, Inc., as its subsidiary in Sunnyvale. This facility is supposed to have begun 16K static RAM (SRAM) production. However, the facility did not have a long life and was closed down in 1986. Finally, Daewoo also set up a subsidiary, ID Focus (IDF), in Santa Clara. IDF was originally set up as a design facility. In addition, however, it has 64K DRAM production capability and has seemed capable of entering the 256K market.

At present, then, Korean semiconductor firms seem to be adopting a strategy very similar to that of their Japanese counterparts. They are complementing their Korean facilities with major investments in design and production sites in the United States. In addition, they are beginning to develop an extensive distribution network in the US.

Major plant construction in Korea

Hyundai, Goldstar, Samsung, and Daewoo announced plans to invest over $1 billion in advanced memory production during the five year period between 1984 and 1988. Samsung completed a VLSI plant at Suwon in 1984. This facility can currently start about 1500 wafers per day, and additional production lines are planned. Production was initiated with 64K DRAMs and 256K production was begun in mid to late 1985.

Goldstar also announced plans to enter 256K production in late 1985. In addition, it established an $18 million R & D center near Seoul which gives the company 5-inch wafer production capability.

Actual production capability took longer to emerge at Hyundai and Daewoo. Both announced plans for 256K production to begin in mid-1986.

Governmental support

For the microelectronics sector, government policy has focused on the promotion of basic research and development. Current tax policy calls for sheltering up to 3 per cent of a company's revenues if these are used for R&D expenditure. The government has also supported the industry through the research institutes described above and is supporting a cooperative research program between leading Korean firms to explore technologies likely to emerge in the next decade.

Country-specific data

Table 3.1 portrays some of the 25 variable values which are used to drive the model in its current form. Data for the three countries have been drawn from a variety of sources, including United Nations and World Bank publications, national statistical abstracts, industry journals, and interviews with industry experts.

A major reason for our inclusion of India in this comparison set is the enormous range in wage levels which it introduces. While our information suggests wage ratios between 2.5 and 3.0 for the US and Korea, the ratios for Korea and India are between 4 and 6. The Indian results should provide an insight into whether labor costs are a major determining factor in the determination of least-cost technology and site choices in semiconductor production. If relatively

TABLE 3.1 *Comparative input prices and change rates: Korea, the US and India*

	US	Korea	India	Japan
Daily wage for operators ($)	80	24	6	68
Daily wage for technicians ($)	160	60	9	150
Daily wage for engineers ($)	200	72	12	180
Working days per year	200	240	220	220
Working hours per day	8	9	8	10
Land price ($'000/acre)	150	150	200	750
Plant constr. price ($/sq.ft.)	100	50	75	95
Clean room constr. price ($/sq.ft.)	600	660	660	660
Interest rate (%)	10	10	10	10

labor-intensive technology is not optimum in India, then it is probably safe to assert that it would not be optimum anywhere.

Our adjustments for working days and hours are drawn from standard sources, and reflect rough averages for industries in the three countries. For plant construction, our numbers reflect adjustments from US values. Calculation of price ratios for important inputs to construction activity leads to an estimate that Korean and Indian plant construction costs are 0.5 and 0.75 (respectively) those of the US. Since the current industry estimate for semiconductor plant construction in the US is $100/sq. ft., we have used these percentages to determine the Korean and Indian costs. Our prices for improved industrial land are currently the most uncertain in the set. They reflect judgmental values, at best. Since clean room construction demands close tolerances and uses specialized skills and materials, we have simply set clean room construction costs for Korea and India at the US value plus a 10 per cent transport markup.

Our interest rate and amortization numbers are set with an eye to preserving comparability for the purposes of these illustrative simulations. We make no attempt to adjust the interest and depreciation rates for local circumstances because we want to highlight the effects of other factors: scale, learning, technology choice, start-up timing, and relative factor costs. In like manner, we have adjusted expected price growth rates for gross observable differences in national rates, but no more than that.

Since we assume that most equipment and speciality supplies for DRAM production are imported by both Korea and India, we have specified a 10 per cent transport markup in both cases.

64K DRAM Simulation Results

We once again consider three technologies: Manual, Semi-Automatic and Automatic (or Robotic). In industry terminology, Semi-automatic technology is the so-called cassette-to-cassette (C-C) technology. Here the wafers to be processed are fed to a workstation in a cassette and the workstation delivers them in a cassette after they have been processed. The handling of the cassettes between stations is done manually. Robotic technology, which is somewhat futuristic (although it has been implemented in a few factories) will not require any human intervention. We also study the effect of scale of production. The usual industry measure is the number of wafers started (or put into the production line) every week.

For a baseline simulation run, we make two deliberately unrealistic assumptions: (1) Korea, the US and India all achieve production start-up in the same quarter; and (2) all three countries have the same learning rates. By controlling for these two variables in the first run, we are simply highlighting the results of yield dynamics, scale, the relative efficiency of different technologies, and variations in input costs.

Robotic Production: Absolute Efficiency?

The results (see Table 3.2) provide a dramatic illustration of the practical importance of factors whose theoretical significance has been discussed, but whose impact could not be assessed in the absence of actual simulation. If our numbers are even approximately correct, then one thing stands out clearly: As long as one country has the resources to move to large-scale Automated or Semi-Automated 64K DRAM production, factor cost advantages will not salvage the position of its competitors. Capital-intensive technologies appear to dominate absolutely because their yield curves are greatly superior. Even in the Indian case, for example, the Manual technology is a distinctly inferior choice.

Moreover, on the assumption that it can actually field the resources necessary for large-scale, cassette-to-cassette installations, India leads the field. Its facility has a delivered unit cost of $0.82 – clearly below the competition in a market where homogeneity and mass ordering requirements assure great sensitivity to slight price differentials.

Thus, in each country the largest-scale most automated technology proves to be the cheapest, and the country with the lowest input costs, India, proves to have the lowest overall costs.

It is important to recall that this result is obtained only when India is able to start production at the same time as the US and also that its learning rate is equivalent to the US rate. Realistically, only US firms have the Automated technology within sight; under that restriction, the US would have the lowest costs with only the Semi-Automated Korean and Indian plants as close competitors.

In this result, then, we see the competitive impact of near-term automation prospects emerge clearly. Our numbers suggest that a move to Robotic production by one country gives it a major competitive advantage, *even if learning rates and start-up dates are identical across countries.*

For Korea (and, indeed, for all developing countries which are much poorer than Korea), these numbers suggest that international competition in advanced electronics may force an unpleasant choice. To compete at all, national producers will have to adopt relatively capital-intensive technologies. Obviously, major sources of employment for the unskilled or semiskilled will have to be found elsewhere, since even the employment which is generated by capital-intensive technologies tends to be heavily weighted toward the upper end of the skill spectrum.

Parametric experiment: The implications for Korea

We next examine the implications of delayed start-up and differences in learning rates. We assume a 4-quarter lag in start-up for Korea and 8-quarter lag for India. In the case of learning rates, we are presently largely in the dark. On the modest assumption that Korean and Indian firms learn at a rate 80 per cent as fast as their US counterparts, the latter experience a modest general rise in the rankings, but can still only compete when they are running Robotic or automated C-C plants. If relative learning drops to 50 per cent, then even Manual US operations start looking relatively competitive.

For the present, then, the most realistic assumptions about the 64K DRAM market lead to simulations which are only mildly encouraging for Korea's prospects. In order to compete successfully with US firms using C-C technology, Korean firms have to move to 5000-start, C-C facilities. If US firms can move to Robotic production (even at the 1500-start scale), then Korean unit costs do not look competitive. If India has the resources to mount a large-scale C-C effort, Korean prospects are doubly dimmed.

All of these results must be seen in context, of course. They have been intended, not to portray the actual competitive situation, but to examine the full spectrum of possibilities which characterize advanced semiconductor production when several technologies exist and potential national competitors have widely varying resource costs. In fact, the actual situation is most accurately characterized by the following summary: despite moves to Semi-Automated production in late 1984 and early 1985, US producers in 64K DRAM production were most strongly represented in the 1500-Start, Manual class – that is at the bottom of the potential cost ranking presented above. Even under the assumption of a 4-quarter start-up lag and a learning adjustment of 0.8, Korean plants using the same scale and

TABLE 3.2 *Competitive cost dynamics in 64K DRAM production when learning rates and production start-up dates are identical*

	India[a] R[b] 5000[c]	Korea R 5000	India C 5000	U.S. R 5000	India R 1500	Korea C 5000	India C 1500	Korea R 1500	India M 5000
1[d]	13.90[e]	14.44	15.66	14.23	15.97	16.31	17.51	16.71	18.90
2	3.62	3.77	4.03	3.78	4.16	4.23	4.52	4.38	4.90
3	2.00	2.09	2.18	2.12	2.29	2.31	2.45	2.43	2.60
4	1.40	1.47	1.54	1.51	1.61	1.64	1.73	1.70	1.80
5	1.13	1.20	1.25	1.24	1.30	1.33	1.41	1.40	1.50
6	0.99	1.04	1.08	1.08	1.12	1.17	1.22	1.21	1.30
7	0.89	0.96	1.00	1.01	1.03	1.08	1.11	1.11	1.20
8	0.84	0.89	0.93	0.95	0.98	1.01	1.05	1.05	1.10
9	0.82	0.87	0.89	0.91	0.93	0.97	1.00	1.01	1.00
10	0.79	0.84	0.87	0.89	0.90	0.95	0.98	0.98	1.00
11	0.77	0.83	0.85	0.88	0.88	0.92	0.96	0.97	1.00
12	0.77	0.82	0.84	0.86	0.87	0.91	0.93	0.95	1.00
13	0.75	0.80	0.83	0.86	0.86	0.90	0.93	0.93	1.00
14	0.75	0.80	0.83	0.85	0.85	0.90	0.92	0.93	1.00
15	0.74	0.80	0.82	0.85	0.85	0.90	0.92	0.93	1.00
16	0.74	0.80	0.82	0.85	0.85	0.90	0.92	0.93	0.90

	Korea C 1500	U.S. C 5000	U.S. R 1500	Korea M 5000	India M 1500	U.S. C 1500	Korea M 1500	U.S. M 5000	U.S. M 1500
1	18.35	16.54	17.08	19.77	21.00	19.28	21.97	20.22	23.10
2	4.78	4.40	4.54	5.16	5.43	5.14	5.73	5.38	6.00
3	2.59	2.45	2.55	2.82	2.96	2.86	3.14	3.02	3.40
4	1.85	1.78	1.83	2.01	2.09	2.08	2.23	2.18	2.50
5	1.50	1.47	1.51	1.62	1.68	1.73	1.81	1.78	2.00
6	1.32	1.31	1.32	1.42	1.46	1.53	1.59	1.58	1.80
7	1.22	1.21	1.21	1.30	1.33	1.42	1.46	1.47	1.60
8	1.14	1.14	1.15	1.22	1.26	1.34	1.35	1.38	1.50
9	1.10	1.10	1.11	1.17	1.20	1.29	1.31	1.33	1.50
10	1.06	1.07	1.08	1.13	1.16	1.26	1.27	1.30	1.50
11	1.05	1.06	1.06	1.12	1.14	1.25	1.26	1.29	1.40
12	1.04	1.05	1.05	1.10	1.12	1.23	1.23	1.26	1.40
13	1.03	1.04	1.04	1.10	1.11	1.23	1.23	1.26	1.40
14	1.02	1.04	1.04	1.09	1.10	1.22	1.23	1.26	1.40
15	1.02	1.04	1.04	1.09	1.10	1.21	1.22	1.25	1.40
16	1.02	1.04	1.04	1.08	1.09	1.22	1.22	1.25	1.40

a Country (Korea, U.S., India).
b Technology (Robotic, Cassette-to-Cassette, Manual).
c Scale (1500/5000 Wafer Starts/Day).
d First columns refer to simulation periods.
e Column entries are delivered costs (in $US) for 64K DRAMS (unit factory cost plus transport to US).

technology were capable of producing 64K DRAMs at substantially lower unit delivered cost. Under somewhat realistic conditions, then, our model suggests that Korean producers were capable of competing effectively against their US counterparts. But a number of other factors have intervened, and we will never know whether that was actually the case. The 256K generation appeared sooner than expected; the price competition became fiercer. The anti-dumping suits against the Japanese and the rise of the Yen made things look brighter. But recent infringement suits against the leading Korean firm, Samsung, have made the picture bleaker.

Is Korea Competitive in 256K DRAM Production?

For the purpose of this discussion, it is useful also to include Japan. Referring back to Table 3.1, we have assumed that labor costs are

TABLE 3.3   *256K DRAM production simulation delivered unit costs for alternative technologies and production sites: 1983–88*

	Japan[a] R^b 5000[c]	U.S. R 5000	Korea R 5000	Japan R 1500	U.S. R 1500	Korea R 1500
1983:1	51.82[d]	–	–	57.61	–	–
1983:2	12.41	–	–	13.82	–	–
1983:3	6.55	–	–	7.31	–	–
1983:4	4.63	52.20	–	5.17	58.65	–
1984:1	3.74	12.60	–	4.18	14.19	–
1984:2	3.24	6.71	–	3.64	7.60	–
1984:3	2.96	4.77	–	3.33	5.41	–
1984:4	2.81	3.87	59.17	3.16	4.39	63.69
1985:1	2.69	3.38	14.13	3.02	3.84	15.23
1985:2	2.61	3.10	7.44	2.94	3.53	8.02
1985:3	2.57	2.96	5.24	2.89	3.37	5.65
1985:4	2.55	2.82	4.21	2.87	3.21	4.56
1986:1	2.53	2.74	3.65	2.86	3.13	3.95
1986:2	2.49	2.69	3.34	2.81	3.08	3.61
1986:3	2.48	2.68	3.16	2.78	3.06	3.42
1986:4	2.48	2.65	3.01	2.79	3.05	3.27
1987:1	2.49	2.62	2.93	2.80	3.00	3.18
1987:2	2.49	2.60	2.88	2.80	2.97	3.12
1987:3	2.48	2.60	2.86	2.80	2.98	3.10
1987:4	2.49	2.60	2.84	2.80	2.98	3.08
1988:1	2.49	2.61	2.79	2.81	2.99	3.02
1988:2	2.50	2.60	2.76	2.82	2.98	2.99
1988:3	2.50	2.60	2.76	2.82	2.98	3.00
1988:4	2.51	2.60	2.77	2.84	2.99	3.00

TABLE 3.3   *(Cont'd)*

	Japan S 5000	Korea S 5000	U.S. S 5000	Japan S 1500	Korea S 1500	Korea S 1500
1983:1	72.23	–	–	79.68	–	–
1983:2	19.88	–	–	21.97	–	–
1983:3	10.04	–	–	11.12	–	–
1983:4	7.19	–	72.95	7.97	–	81.00
1984:1	5.75	–	20.36	6.39	–	22.67
1984:2	5.13	–	10.44	5.70	–	11.66
1984:3	4.64	–	7.57	5.15	–	8.46
1984:4	4.39	79.98	6.12	4.88	85.27	6.84
1985:1	4.16	21.90	5.49	4.63	23.38	6.15
1985:2	4.10	11.00	4.98	4.57	11.75	5.59
1985:3	4.03	7.84	4.73	4.50	8.39	5.31
1985:4	3.98	6.26	4.50	4.44	6.70	5.06
1986:1	3.92	5.57	4.45	4.38	5.96	5.00
1986:2	3.93	5.01	4.38	4.39	5.37	4.93
1986:3	3.94	4.74	4.32	4.4	5.07	4.87
1986:4	3.90	4.48	4.26	4.35	4.82	4.81
1987:1	3.91	4.41	4.27	4.36	4.74	4.82
1987:2	3.92	4.34	4.28	4.37	4.66	4.83
1987:3	3.92	4.27	4.22	4.39	4.59	4.77
1987:4	3.93	4.21	4.23	4.40	4.53	4.78
1988:1	3.94	4.22	4.24	4.41	4.53	4.79
1988:2	3.95	4.22	4.25	4.42	4.54	4.80
1988:3	3.96	4.16	4.25	4.43	4.47	4.81
1988:4	3.97	4.17	4.26	4.45	4.48	4.82

[a] Country (Korea, US, Japan)
[b] Technology (Robotic, Cassette-to-Cassette, Manual)
[c] Scale (1500/5000 Wafer Starts/Day)
[d] Column entries are delivered costs (in $US) for 64K DRAMS (unit factory cost plus transport to US)

almost as high as in the US, construction costs are higher (when land costs are taken into account), and wage/cost growth rates are somewhat higher than in the US. Japan's interest rate is set at 10 per cent for this simulation in order to highlight the impact of the factors which have been under discussion. In fact, it might be reasonable to set the Japanese rate somewhat lower.

The simulations above illustrated that relative start-up dates and learning rates have major dynamic impacts on competitiveness in advanced electronics production. In both dimensions, Korean firms entered the 256K market with some disadvantage in comparison with US firms, and clear disadvantages in comparison with Japanese competitors. As we have indicated throughout, relative learning rates remain problematic, and we can only attach some confidence to the weak assertion that Korean firms do not have faster learning rates than US and Japanese firms. With respect to start-up dates, the situation is much clearer.

By the end of 1984, Japanese firms were fully ramped up for 256K production and output was still growing by nearly 100 per cent per quarter. US firms began about 4 quarters behind (Japanese firms actually began shipping in sampling quantities in mid-1983), but by the end of 1984 they were also showing signs of full preparation for mass production. The importance of these time profiles in the current context is their contrast with Korean entry dates.

The conclusion seems unavoidable that by the fast-moving standards of DRAM production, Korean firms entered this market quite late and with relatively less experience than their counterparts in Japan and the United States. Samsung and Goldstar had some experience in 64K DRAM production and may therefore have had learning rates not too far behind those of their Japanese and US competitors. Hyundai and Daewoo on the other hand, had no previous experience.

In our simulations, we assume that US, Japanese and Korean learning rates are identical. This is obviously an assumption which is very favorable to Korea. Our specification of start-up dates reflects actual experience. Again, our assumptions are relatively favorable to Korea, since a 10-quarter lag might be considered a more accurate characterization of Japan's headstart.

There is little ambiguity in the ordering of results. For Robotic technology, the ordering is consistently Japan – US – Korea, with all 5000 wafer-start plants ultimately out-performing their 1500-start counterparts.

For Semi-Automated Plants, the ultimate ordering is Japan – Korea – US, with 5000-start plants again turning in a superior performance.[16] Though the Robotic technology used here has not been thought to exist presently in the US, except perhaps at IBM facilities and pilot plants of major producers such as Intel and Motorola, such technology has probably been coming onstream in Japan. As in the 64K case, it is clear what will happen to the competitive environment when one producer begins output from large-scale Robotic plants. Absolute efficiency is even more pronounced here than in the 64K case. A Robotic Japan can clearly dominate this market, and our best present information suggests that the only hope of US and Korean competitors is to emulate.

In evaluating the simulation outcomes, it is extremely important to note that ultimate Korean costs may not be very informative as a guide to competitive outcomes. The Korean plants come onstream eight quarters into the simulation, and their unit costs remain considerably higher than those of the US and Japanese plants for much of the simulation. In the case of 1500-start Semi-Automated plants, for example, Korean delivered unit costs do not drop below those of the US until the first quarter of 1987. The 256K market "peaked" by 1987, and 1 megabit DRAMs started appearing. Downward pressure on the market price of 256K chips will continue as their moving "sales window" closes. By 1987, it seems entirely plausible to assert that most of the profits in 256K production were long since made. If our numbers are even roughly correct, then an unfortunate conclusion for Korea seems clear. For semi-automated plants (the only kind currently under operation in Korea), the price/cost ratio probably never even got close to 1. Early-entering Japanese and US firms made money in the first few years, as exploitation of relatively inelastic demand left the price/cost margin comfortably above 1. By the first quarter of 1986, only Robotic plants were still making profits; by early 1987, all profits basically evaporated. For Semi-Automatic plants, the denouement came much earlier. The Japanese ceased making money in early 1986, and the Americans arrived at a unitary ratio in mid-late 1985.[17]

Insofar as our model is correctly specified, and insofar as our input cost data are roughly correct, it is quite difficult to see how Korean enterprises could have made any money in 256K DRAM production. It may well be the case, however, that they see participation (and losses) in this market as prerequisite for early entry and ultimate success in the 1 megabit chip market.

DID THE JAPANESE DUMP SEMICONDUCTORS?

Although our information about technology and costs in Japanese firms is pretty good, we cannot claim that we can pinpoint production costs by the "typical" Japanese semiconductor firm exactly. We have therefore simulated Japanese costs under a range of assumptions about process yield rates and factor prices. In the figure which follows, we present the simulated price/cost ratio paths for the extreme assumptions which seem plausible. Our "high" ratio path looks quite similar to the path for the typical US firm which we portrayed earlier. To generate this path, we have assumed US-level process yield rates, a US learning speed, and labor costs at the upper limit by current Japanese standards. We have also assumed a typical US production scale – 1500 silicon wafer starts per day, and typical current US cassette-to-cassette technology.

Our "low" ratio path adopts assumptions which may well provide a better reflection of current Japanese reality. We have talked to no industry expert, either in the US or Japan, who thinks that Japanese process yield rates and learning speeds are at parity with those of their US counterparts. Rather, the consensus is that yield rates are substantially higher and learning speeds somewhat higher. In addition, our interviews in Japan persuaded us that it would be a mistake to assume that assembly labor in Japanese semiconductor firms should be priced at the going wage for full-time male workers. Rather, much of this labor is provided by females, many of them married, who work part-time at assembly points located in suburban or rural areas. The consensus among industry experts in Japan is that the wages paid to these female workers are quite low. Many Japanese firms are in the process of shifting to highly-automated, large-scale production facilities. We have therefore calculated our "low" ratio path on the assumption of 5000 wafer starts per day and "Robotic" technology.

Figure 3.4 traces out simulated Japanese price/cost ratios (by quarter) for the two sets of assumptions. Our estimates suggest that Japanese firms could justifiably have been accused of "dumping" under existing US law only if the "worst case" scenario is adopted – that is, the case which corresponds quite closely to then-existing production conditions for US firms. When superior Japanese yield rates, learning speeds, automation, and scale are combined with a more realistic estimate of assembly labor costs, we can see that Japanese firms were just about breaking even after the "price crash" of late 1985. The slump in semiconductor demand clearly precipitated a ferocious price war among Japanese suppliers. Our numbers suggest, however, that even the post-crash price could plausibly be termed a "break even" point.

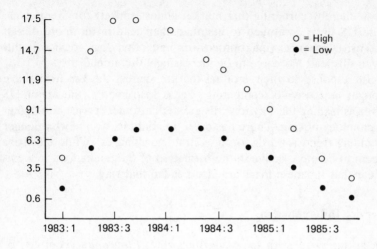

FIGURE 3.4   *Simulated price/cost ratios for Japanese semiconductor producers*

FUTURE DIRECTIONS

In this section we examine new developments that are currently determining the pattern of technological evolution in the semiconductor industry. While the relentless drive towards greater miniaturization will continue to have some of its past momentum, new forces are emerging which are likely to change the pattern and speed of technical change. The forces include: (1) movement towards greater service and customer orientation; (2) higher prices for technology sales; (3) greater emphasis on strategic alliances for technology and market sharing; and (4) greater US government involvement in protecting the US industry. We have already discussed the dumping issue and shall focus on the other three dimensions of change.

The nature of competition in the semiconductor industry was shaped during the last decade mainly by the aggressive price competition of the Japanese firms. We described this process in previous sections: The large price-cost margins enjoyed by the US firms in the 16K and 64K DRAM markets induced and allowed the Japanese to compete in these markets. The Japanese then built large production capacitites in the 256K DRAM market and kept prices much closer to cost, thereby cornering that market almost entirely for themselves. The US firms continued to maintain their lead in the more design intensive products (microprocessors and other logic devices); but even this lead has come to be increasingly threatened.

In response to their eroding market shares, the US firms have sought new ways of competing. Texas Instruments, the major US firm, is leading the way towards greater customer service and higher technology pricing. There has been, in addition, a somewhat longer standing trend towards forming strategic alliances. While US firms seem to be more active in the formation of these alliances, it seems clear that Japanese firms are also headed that way.

Service Differentiation

In an interview with the trade magazine, *Electronics* (February 3, 1986, p. 18), Jerry R. Junkins, the President of Texas Instruments, is reported to have said that he was "asking TI divisions to develop 'much closer customer relationships'. Service "dominates our thinking now ... It is no longer sufficient for a company to have a corner on the technology and the cost." There are two strands of TI's service differentiation strategy. One relates to its "commodity" products and the other to its customized products.

"Commodity" products

Commodity products are those that are produced using mass production techniques: The physical aspects of the product are not tailored to customer requirements. According to one recent report, TI has extended its service differentiation strategy over its commodity logic products, which represent 70 per cent of TI's unit volumes.[18]

There are two main features of the TI strategy: Increasing the share of its customers' accounts and eventually achieving sole-supplier status. "TI believes that getting closer to the customer would help it forecast demand better, and would allow delivery guarantees. Accurate forecasts would stabilize business swings for TI."[19]

In return for this close relationship, TI offers the customer the advantage of inventory reduction. The main program in this regard is referred to as the 100 per cent on-time program. The emphasis is on guaranteeing delivery in the time window specified. According to TI executives, it is important for cost reduction that delivery be guaranteed even if that implies lengthening the time window of delivery: "...some customers want extremely small windows – two and five days. A lot of suppliers will try to meet that, but they ship only 80 per cent to 85 per cent on time. What good is that? It's better for the customer if you ship 100 per cent on time to a wider window, say 15 days."[20] Eventually the goal at TI is to shorten the window and to deliver 100 per cent accurately.

In order to achieve the quick and accurate response, TI has installed a major systems infrastructure.

TI starts with the data-communication network. At last count, the web ties together 650-odd IBM mainframes and regional or level-2 computers, such as the IBM 43XX series; and about 14,000 of TI's own professional computers. That kind of resource capability is difficult to duplicate. In a sense, then, TI's sheer size is one reason that it could pull this off. Ideally, what TI would like to set up is a system capability so that an order entered anywhere in the world would dynamically alert the planning system. That, in turn, would query available requirements, factor in the finished-goods inventory and work out a delivery schedule. TI maintains that this level of capability is likely to be set in place within the next year.[21]

The above developments (and the likelihood that other US and Japanese firms will follow) have important implications. First, to the extent that the major existing producers will try to gain the right to supply the entire requirements of individual customers, the need for second-sourcing will decline. Second-sourcing has been a major source of stability for the buyers of semiconductors. It has allowed them to place orders with two or more suppliers in order to meet their requirements. Second-sourcing has also been a method of entry for latecomers. The elimination of second-sourcing could increase the entry barriers in the forthcoming product generations. Secondly, the resources required to maintain captive customers are, as described above, becoming increasingly large. The need for quick response to customer needs will require not merely an improved communication network but also more varied and extensive production facilities.

The second feature of TI's "commodity" strategy is to guarantee that "incoming inspection and its associated costs can be dispensed with; that board- and system-level rework can be eliminated and field failures reduced".[22] This again places a premium on large internal resources for the firm and points in the direction of increasing advantage for large firms.

The essence of the TI "commodity" strategy is to achieve a general saving for the customer in terms of the inventory he holds and in terms of his requirement to inspect the product supplied. Does this saving represent a saving from the larger societal point of view? In other words, would the savings of the TI customers be greater than the extra costs to TI? The answer to this question will have to wait for a careful empirical assessment. It is our view, at this stage, that macro (or overall) savings in inventories and testing resources will indeed occur, at least in the initial phase; however, the process will also generate greater monopoly power for firms like TI.

Customization strategy

All of the above is relevant for the customization strategy. In addition, customization is to be promoted through opening several service centers where customers can design their products in association with TI staff. The designs are then to be transmitted to some central facility which will allocate prototype production to a production facility. The prototype is then tested and the revised design is to be sent for final production.

Again, the success of such a strategy will depend upon the availability of resources to open a large number of service centers and the *creation* of demand for customized products even from small users. There clearly would be large economies of scale in such a strategy.

It has been the hope of small firms in the US and of firms from middle-income countries such as Korea and Taiwan that the custom market would provide "niches" which they could exploit. If the above trends are to be believed, it will be more economical to produce *several* semi-custom and custom product lines since that will provide a better utilization of design and production resources. However, the production of several production lines will also increase investment requirements and hence increase entry barriers.

Price of Technology

In a recent litigation, Texas Instruments claimed that eight Japanese and one Korean company, Samsung, infringed its DRAM technology patents.[23] TI also filed a related action with the International Trade

Commission (ITC) seeking relief from injury due to patent infringement. On the past alleged infringements, most Japanese companies have settled with Texas Instruments by paying about $100 million. Samsung, which did not settle out of court, has been found guilty by the ITC of infringing on patents held by Texas Instruments and has consequently been banned from selling DRAMs in the United States. The ban will probably not materialize because TI has granted Samsung temporary licences to its patent and it is expected that licensing on a more permanent basis will follow. Norman H. Neureiter, TI vice president, has said: "It is impossible to make a DRAM today without drawing on the technology described or covered in our patents in some way" ... Neureiter has added that "TI has had patent cross-licencing pacts with many Japanese companies, but all expired without being renewed."[24]

At the same time, TI is now demanding a 13 per cent royalty, a hefty jump from the existing norm of one per cent. Thus, TI's success in defending its patents will mean that either the Japanese and Korean firms will be barred from the US market or they will have to pay very large royalties.

Perhaps even more importantly,

TI has quietly filed over the past year a barrage of patent applications in the U.S. and overseas intended to cover the most feasible approaches to three-dimensional structures for storage cells. A 3-d storage cell is considered essential to reducing the array areas of DRAMs reaching densities of 4 Mb and beyond ... During the research phase of the 4-Mb trench-transistor cell, TI's semiconductor laboratory explored 15 to 20 possible approaches. "There was a patent a week coming out of there," recalls Greg Armstrong, manager of CMOS technology in the Advanced Development Division of the Semiconductor Group. "I would suspect we have covered just about every possible alternative of putting a transistor in a trench for a single cell. There will be a lot of people frustrated – every way they turn, there will be a TI patent."[25]

These developments raise a number of important issues. First, it appears that there is a new awareness of the importance of intellectual property.[26] Secondly, although intellectual property is clearly seen as important, it is not clear that the system has developed adequate methods of pricing it. What, for example, should be the appropriate price of technology? Our basic conclusion is that there is probably no appropriate price. It is not easy to forecast the expected returns from a new technology. In the past, the seller (such as TI) has underestimated the technology potential. However, charging a very high price may not be the right response from the private or social view point. Partly, the difficulty is going to be in ascertaining "how high is high". TI's decision to charge 13 per cent royalty does not lead to a sacred number. Why not charge 10 per cent or 20 per cent, for example? In the next section, we suggest that in fact the purchase and sale of technology may decrease; instead, firms will probably increasingly resort to forming strategic alliances to jointly exploit technology.

Formation of Strategic Alliances

There has been a definite trend in a number of major industries towards closer cooperation between the leading firms. These alliances include international collaborations. In the age of exploding information, a curious phenomenon has occured. Exploitation of information requires greater specialization. A firm operating in a particular market segment now has to devote greater resources to deepening and broadening its technological information, lest a competitor discover and exploit a competitive weapon. However, in seeking deeper knowledge in its area of specialization, a firm acquires certain general principles of operation which can be exploited across different sectors. This provides the motivation for forming alliances. Thus, increasing information has had the effect of increasing the economies of scale in the use of information.

A recently formed alliance brings together utterly different skills. Counterpoint Computers, a San Jose venture, has forged ties with AT&T, Kyocera (Japan) and British and Commonwealth Shipping. "The startup will get help from Kyocera Corp., the world's largest supplier of ceramic packages for integrated circuits, in packaging its systems. AT&T will be an original-equipment-manufacturer customer as well as a technical partner, especially in the area of Unix, the operating system under which Counterpoint's engines will run. British and Commonwealth Shipping Co., a London-based conglomerate with high-technology operations, will provide an entry into the European market."[27]

In the semiconductor business, Advanced Micro Devices (US) has recently formed an alliance with Sony (Japan). Under the agreement, "AMD and Sony Corp. will share design and production technology on 'the next generation of certain types of ICs ...'[28] Sony's strength lies in its 'systems experience' (or the ability to design and produce complete systems, mainly in consumer electronics); AMD is strong in design and processing of VLSI. For AMD, the alliance allows greater return on its VLSI technology through extending its participation into consumer markets."[29]

While the various antidumping suits have got tremendous publicity, it is our judgement that the competitive changes being brought about by service differentiation, rising technology prices and formation of strategic alliances are perhaps the more critical ones. The changes being wrought in the semiconductor industry bear a remarkable resemblance to those in the textile/garment and automobile industries. In these sectors as well, US firms are attempting to respond to import pressure through service differentiation (particularly quick response) and increased automation.

This suggests that a new era of competition is opening up. All factors point to an increase in concentration of production in the near future. Only the large firms will be able to afford the data communications network and infrastructure support necessary for customization strategies. The potential breakdown in the market for technology will prevent the growth of new firms and of firms with limited R&D resources. Scale economies in information use will also lead to bigger firms. What impact all this will have on the pace of technical change is, of course, the big question. Over the next few years, as the various adjustments are made to the strategies we have outlined, we have no reason to believe that there will be any slowing down. Thereafter, that is once the new structure matures, the pace of change is likely to slow down.

APPENDIX 3: MODELING COMPETITIVE COST DYNAMICS IN DRAM PRODUCTION

This Appendix contains a description of our dynamic costing model for semiconductor memories. The model has the following capabilities: For a particular chip type (e.g. 64K), it accepts any number of production vectors for model plants which integrate the four essential processes in semiconductor production: wafer processing; wafer probe; assembly; and testing. Each process is modeled separately. Thus, alternative technologies at differing scales and factor intensities can be introduced. The model also accepts relevant input cost data for any number of countries, and has been designed to accept country-specific learning-rate adjustments. It allows for estimated increase rates in unit input costs by country. Countries can enter the competition during the first period, or in any subsequent period.

The model is driven through successive periods by evolving yield rates, input prices, and product prices. In each period, the model calculates the costs associated with all possible technologies for each country. For different technologies in competing countries, learning curve effects can be realized at differential rates. Unit costs fall at different speeds toward long-run asymptotic values determined by technology parameters and local input costs. Unit profitability by country is indexed by the ratio of the prevailing market price and local unit costs.

In each period, the market price for a particular DRAM type is determined by two factors. For the period when the chip it self dominates the market (in the sense that its price-per-kilobit is lower than that of its predecessors and/or successors), its own historical price trend is used as the basis for projection. During the period when its successor is appearing, its price is forced to match the long-run decline in minimum price per kilobit. This use of the long-run price reduction profile simulates the increasing market pressure which will be felt by producers of a particular DRAM as more powerful chips emerge.

DATA ACQUISITION

For this exercise, we have engaged in an intensive investigation of the DRAM production technologies which currently exist or will soon exist. Because the market for 16K DRAM chips is moving toward insignificance, and Korea has obviously opted for a commitment to 64K and 256K production, we have focused our modeling exercise on the latter two DRAMs. It should be emphasized at the outset, however, that our model is perfectly general in nature. It will accept information on possible technologies for the production of any DRAMs or, indeed, for any VLSI products (SRAMs, EPROMs, Microprocessors, etc.).

We have been quite fortunate in our dealings with semiconductor engineers, managers, industry consultants, and interested academics. The semiconductor industry is fast-moving, and sufficiently complex that no one pretends to have full knowledge at any point in time. As researchers, we have therefore encountered a very gratifying openness which has allowed us to make good progress on the characterization of technology.

At the beginning of the interview process, our basic tools were a detailed set of questions about the industry and a set of tentative technology estimates which were derived from reading the technical literature and industry publications. Of particular help in this regard were Finan and Lamond (1985); Sze (1983); ICE (1980–85), and *Semiconductor International* (1985). Armed with these estimates, we held numerous discussions with academic experts, engineers, consultants, and industry people in New England, California's Silicon Valley, and Arizona. Since these are three of the top four sites for semiconductor-related activity in the US (the fourth being Texas), we think that our coverage in the US has been relatively comprehensive.

During a 1985 research trip to Japan, we continued our interviews with industry specialists, consultants, and academic experts. We received particularly useful cooperation from Hitachi and Applied Materials Japan, which is one of the foremost suppliers of capital equipment to the Japanese semiconductor industry. In the course of our interviews, we received additional confirmation of our working hypotheses about Japanese learning speeds and yield rates.

Through a process of continued discussion and refinement, we have developed a set of technology estimates for DRAM production which seem relatively reliable. Our effort has also derived benefit from the exceptional generosity of some industry consultants. A particularly valuable contribution has been made by Mr Howard Dicken, one of the premier consultants to the semiconductor industry.[30] Mr Dicken has developed a computer model which simulates the technical details of semiconductor production under widely differing technical assumptions (e.g. operations scale; feature size; number of masks, wafer size, die area, etc.). His model incorporates experiences derived from his study of numerous production facilities in the US, Brazil, Korea, and elsewhere.

Mr Dicken has generously allowed us to work with the actual code of his program, and we have been able to incorporate several of his technical process equations into our own model. This has been particularly useful in our treatment of yield determination by process stage, since yields are arguably the most important "driving force" in semiconductor production.

MODEL STRUCTURE

Our model operates according to the following schema:

Data Input

The model is constructed to operate on standard technology vectors, which have been distilled from our interviews and reading of the technical literature. These vectors are standardized on yield rates which characteristically prevail after production has been in progress for six quarters (18 months). The user of the model can choose initially between analysis of 64K or 256K DRAM production. Once this choice has been made, the model displays the standard technology vectors and allows any desired modifications to be made. This allows for experiments with hypothetical alternative technologies.

At present, we have six standard technologies for 64K DRAM production and four technologies for 256K production. In each case, variety is introduced by significant variations in scale and degree of automation. For 64K operations, three levels of automation are introduced: "Manual" (which reflects typical US practice recently and is still employed in many plants); "Cassette-to-Cassette", which automates wafer fabrication substantially and improves yields by eliminating much manual transfer of wafers between production stations; and "Robotic", which reflects the current view of industry experts concerning the most automated form of production which would be feasible.

For each of these technologies, two typical plant scales are included. The first, 1500 wafer starts per day, reflects typical industry practice for this stage of VLSI. For contrast, technology vectors for 5000-wafer-start plants are also included. Plants on this scale are judged to be near the feasible maximum at present, although some industry experts are beginning to discuss 10 000-start plants as automation proceeds. A 5000-start plant is very large: Even a program as ambitious as Korea's current project would involve the construction of only a handful of plants of this size.

Standard Technologies: 64K DRAM Production

Table A.3.1 displays the standard production vectors which provide the starting point for model operations in the case of 64K production.

TABLE A.3.1 *Standard technologies for 64K DRAM production*

	Manual		Cassette to Cassette		Robotic	
Capacity (Starts/day)	1500	5000	1500	5000	1500	5000
Wafer processing (125 mm.)						
Yield rate (%)	80	80	88	88	93	93
No. of operators	220	725	150	495	100	330
No. of technicians	60	120	70	140	100	200
No. of engineers	57	115	60	120	80	160
Capital ($ million)	35	101	40	116	50	145
Materials ($ per wafer)	75	75	60	60	60	60
Wafer probe						
Yield rate (%)	40	40	45	45	50	50
No. of operators	30	90	30	90	25	75
No. of technicians	5	10	5	10	8	16
No. of engineers	5	10	5	10	7	14
Capital ($ million)	0	0	0	0	0	0
Materials ($ per wafer)	0	0	0	0	0	0
Assembly						
Yield rate (%)	92	92	92	92	97	97
No. of operators	210	630	210	630	100	300
No. of technicians	18	36	18	36	40	80
No. of engineers	17	34	17	34	30	60
Capital ($ million)	3	9	3	9	15	45
Materials ($ per die)	.10	.10	.10	.10	.10	.10
Testing						
Yield Rate (%)	75	75	75	75	90	90
No. of operators	90	270	90	270	60	180
No. of technicians	15	30	15	30	18	36
No. of engineers	15	30	15	30	17	34
Capital ($ million)	8	24	8	24	20	50
Materials ($ per die)	0	0	0	0	0	0
Building requirements						
Lot size (acres)	6	6.3	6	6.3	6	6.3
Building size (sq.ft.)	50000	53000	50000	53000	50000	53000
Clean room (sq.ft.)	12000	13000	12000	13000	12000	13000

The numbers reflect the operation of certain basic economic forces which have been discussed in previous sections. These forces will be considered using columns 1, 3, and 5, since they reflect changes in technology but not in scale. From Manual to Cassette-to-Cassette operation, the only changes are in the wafer processing stage. As previously noted, wafers are better protected at transfer points in the latter mode. As a result, characteristic yield in the 6th operation quarter rises from 80 percent to 88 percent when Cassette-to-Cassette technology is adopted. Associated capital requirements increase, as do requirements for technicians and engineers. The production engineers whom we have interviewed have stressed the importance of skilled technicians in this process. As highly sophisticated equipment becomes common, the technicians become increasingly important as providers of support, maintenance, repairs, etc. They undoubtedly form a key element in the intellectual infrastructure which must underlie competition in advanced electronics production.

While requirements for technical skills increase, operator requirements decrease, because the cassette handling technology reduces the need for manual operations. Material costs associated with wafer-handling decline, and probe yield increases somewhat because wafer handling has introduced fewer inpurities. In summary, the introduction of Cassette-to-Cassette technology involves some increase in capital- and skill-intensity, with somewhat higher expenditures for equipment. Compensating cost reductions are realized through higher yield profiles and a reduction in the number of operators required for wafer fabrication.

In the case of robotic technology, which is at the frontier of current thinking about feasible processes, the shifts described above are further accentuated. In this case, however, the change is felt in all four processing steps. Capital expenditure at each stage jumps dramatically, more technicians and engineers are required, and all yield rates improve substantially. According to industry experts whom we have interviewed, the overhead associated with plant size does not change appreciably during this transition.

While columns 1, 3, and 5 of Table A.3.1 reflect changes in technology, columns 2, 4, and 6 represent changes in scale. The evidence currently available suggests that some scale economies are realized for each technology, but that they are relatively modest. As a general rule, it can be said that operator requirements increase in direct proportion to output, equipment requirements increase slightly less than proportionally, and technican/engineer requirements increase much less than proportionally. The consensus of industry experts is that plant and clean room requirements increase, but only slightly.

Standard Technologies: 256K Production

In a qualitative sense, the relations among 256K technology vectors reflect the factors which have been discussed in the 64K case. Three features are particularly noteworthy. First, the entire process is much more capital- and skill-intensive than 64K processes at equivalent scale. The Semi-Automated technology for 256K production is more automated than the Robotic version of 64K production. The same increase in intensity holds for the skill structure of the required labor force. Despite these shifts, characteristic yield rates in wafer processing and wafer probe at the six-quarter point are considerably lower than in the 64K case.

The reasons for this deterioration in yield performance are technical and have already been discussed in detail. Characteristic feature size declines from 3 to 2 microns; die size increases from around 35 000 square mils to 55 000. Yields decline substantially in consequence, and at any point in time the cost per good die in production is substantially above that for 64K DRAMs. Of course, the 256K chip has ultimately greater economic appeal because it has a cost/performance advantage at any level below four times the unit cost of the 64K chip.

Scale shifts in the 256K case have consequences which parallel those in 64K production. The relevant inputs are displayed in Table A.3.2. Operator requirement elasticity is 1; the equipment requirement elasticity is modestly below 1; technician/engineer requirements have elasticities substantially below one; and plant/clean room requirements have elasticities near zero.

For 64K and 256K operations, then, the standard production vectors set the stage for the dynamic cost simulations. The system is affected by three major "drivers": Yield rates, which are sensitive to technology choice; scale economies; and input substitution possibilities. In a static sense, the choice of optimum technology depends on yields, labor costs by skill class, capital costs, and the prevailing interest rate. Our problem, however, is not static. Yield rates adjust rapidly during the process of production, and "downstream" labor requirements in assembly and final testing change as more good die are emitted by the wafer fabrication process. At the same time, competition from other producers and (ultimately) more advanced chips is steadily driving down the market price of the output. It is therefore clear that the optimum technology can only be chosen after all these dynamics have been taken into account.

TABLE A.2   *Standard technologies for 64K DRAM production*

	Semi-Automatic		Robotic	
Capacity (wafers/day)	1500	5000	1500	5000
Wafer processing				
Yield rate (%)	71	71	85	85
No. of operators	84	280	40	130
No. of technicians	112	240	170	350
No. of engineers	84	160	100	200
Capital ($ million)	51	172	65	220
Materials ($ per wafer)	95	95	74	74
Wafer probe				
Yield rate (%)	24	24	35	35
No. of operators	30	90	25	75
No. of technicians	5	15	5	15
No. of engineers	5	15	5	15
Capital ($ million)	0	0	0	0
Materials ($ per wafer)	0	0	0	0
Assembly				
Yield rate (%)	92	92	97	97
No. of operators	110	330	50	150
No. of technicians	9	18	18	36
No. of engineers	9	18	18	36
Capital ($ million)	3	9	15	45
Materials ($ per die)	.10	.10	.10	.10
Testing				
Yield Rate (%)	80	80	95	95
No. of operators	50	150	30	90
No. of technicians	10	20	10	20
No. of engineers	10	20	10	20
Capital ($ million)	16	48	40	120
Materials ($ per die)	0	0	0	0
Building requirements				
Lot size (acres)	8.5	8.9	7	7.4
Building size (sq.ft.)	71000	74000	60000	63000
Clean room (sq.ft.)	15000	16000	15000	16000

Economic Data

Because the competitive cost model treats semiconductor production at a detailed level, its requirements for specific input price data are also relatively exacting. The requirements can be seen, in fact, by reviewing Table A.3.2. For competitor countries (or, for that matter, firms – the model will operate on any competitive terrain) average daily wage rates are needed for three labor skill classes: operators, technicians, and engineers. Since most relevant equipment is for sale in international markets, equipment prices outside Japan and the US can simply be adjusted for transport costs. The same thing is true for materials prices, since the relevant materials are highly sophisticated inputs and have not (until recently, anyway) been produced outside the OECD countries. Finally, information on the cost of appropriate industrial sites is required, as well as average prices for constructing plants and clean room facilities. Because all capital purchases must be carried in long-term accounts, local interest rates must also be factored in.

For a dynamic analysis of cost-competitiveness, it is appropriate to include estimates of annual change rates in some prices as well as their current levels. In Korea, for example, wages for workers at all skill levels have been rising much faster than those of their US counterparts. Japanese industrial site prices, which are already far higher than those in the US, have been rising at a relatively rapid rate. Since 10 percent growth in a number implies doubling at seven-year intervals, rapid price increases must be taken into account.

MODEL OPERATIONS

Yield Rates

In our investigation of semiconductor industry dynamics, the critical role of learning embodied in yield improvements seems clear. In order to allow for a comprehensive consideration of yield impacts, the model incorporates yield curves in a highly flexible way. The best current estimates of experts have been incorporated into the yield model for each process step, but adjustments must be made for shifts in all the time profiles with rising capital intensity. The model handles this by shifting the entire yield curve (which is technically specified as a function of experience and technical chip and wafer characteristics) so that its 6-quarter level matches that of the technology vector. All other yield numbers are adjusted proportionally.

For 64K DRAM production, then, there are many yield curves. The wafer processing and probe yield curves are adjusted for changes from Manual to Cassette-to-Cassete (C-C) technology, and again for the transition from the latter to Robotic technology. Assembly and final test yield curves are adjusted for the transition from C-C to Robotic technology. In the 256K case, all four process yield curves are adjusted upward for the shift from Semi-Automatic to Robotic technology.

The model also allows for international differences in learning rates. At this time, any quantification of such differences must be regarded as highly speculative. Academic economists and management experts are so far from hard evidence in this sphere that the subject is not even controversial yet. Since yield curves are central to an understanding of competition in this (and undoubtedly other) high technology fields, we can confidently predict that the current silence on this subject will soon be broken. For the moment, however, we can only supply educated guesses and parametric experiments.

At present, the informal industry consensus seems to be as follows: Across countries, learning rates do differ as a function of industry experience, skill levels, and engineering/scientific education levels. The consensus among those we have interviewed is that Japanese enterprises have somewhat higher learning rates than their US counterparts. Korean enterprises, on the other hand, are generally supposed to have somewhat lower learning rates because of differences in production experience, embodied education, and support infrastructure. Most poorer developing countries are supposed to have much lower learning rates.

The model allows for these differences to be quantified by specifying national rates as percentages of the US rate. The yield curves are related to duration of process since start-up on the assumption of steady activity.[31] An adjustment of 0.5 in this index system would imply learning at half the US rate – yield rates in the country in question would take eight quarters to reach their four-quarter levels in US firms. Once national adjustment factors are specified, the model re-standardizes all technology-specific yield curves for lead/lag relationships with US standard yield curves.

It should also be noted that this allowance for learning differences permits introduction of differences due to earlier experience in DRAM production. The consensus of industry experts is that experienced firms start higher-capacity DRAM production with a significant learning advantage. As production proceeds, their yield rates move up more quickly because their operators, technicians, and engineers know how to go about "tweaking the process", in the words of one consultant interviewed. In simulating cost paths for 256K DRAM production, prior experience in 64K DRAM production can be registered as an adjustment to relative learning speed.

Intertemporal Input Adjustments

Once all yield curves have been adjusted for differing technologies and national learning rates, the model begins its operation by "backcasting" to process start-up conditions. This step is necessary because the initial technology vectors are presented for modification at a point in the yield curve which corresponds approximately to six quarters of steady activity by a US firm at the rated wafer-start level (adjusted for capacity utilization). Labor requirements for the assembly and test phases are set at appropriate levels for the number of good die yielded by wafer processing at this point in production history.

Once the input requirements have been shifted (or not, as the case may be) by the user, the model adjusts yield rates backward (and forward) in simulation time according to a rather complex set of multiplicative and exponential relations which are dictated by the interaction among wafer/die surface geometries, expected wafer impurity levels, feature sizes (in microns), mask numbers, and production experience. As the simulation moves backward towards start-up, probe yields decline rather spectacularly and process and test yields also move downward significantly. This adjusts for the fact that at start-up, the number of good dies produced by wafer processing is extremely small.

By taking this into account, the model is able to adjust "upstream" assembly and test input requirements for minimal throughput. By the same token, "downstream" assembly and test inputs are increased as good die output improves. The model generates estimated increases in inputs according to the same logic which holds for scale increases between technology vectors: Operators increase proportionally with throughput, as do material inputs; engineers and technicians increase, but at a substantially slower rate. By adjusting input requirements in this manner, the model preserves realism: full unit start-up costs are lower than simple back-casting of yield rates would suggest, while unit cost declines with increasing process experience are not as steep as the changing yield rates themselves would imply.

Market Entry Delays

A critical problem for potential competitors in the DRAM market is the implication of alternative start-up dates for production. The pros and cons of leadership and follower status have been discussed extensively earlier. Because this factor is so important, the model has been designed to allow for variable market entry dates by different national competitors. In the model equations, the whole production history of countries which start up after the first period is simply moved forward in time relative to competitor nations. All yield curve and input adjustments are preserved, but all are shifted in time to dovetail with the specified retardation factor.

Capital Accounting

Although the initial technology vectors specify full capital costs by process step for ease of interpretation, it is clear that these costs should be amortized over substantial periods in a sensible cost model. Capital costing is never easy, and when differences in national circumstances may be taken into account, the subject becomes complex indeed. Under ideal circumstances, a sophisticated capital costing model such as that proposed by Hall and Jorgenson (1967) would be employed. We plan to give further attention to this problem in future research (see Downs, 1986, for a criticism of the Hall and Jorgenson approach). For the moment capital costs are handled using straight-line depreciation. The model allows depreciation factors to be set by the user, but its default conventions are 5 years for equipment, 10 years for clean room construction, and 20 years for land and plant.

Interest charges must be considered along with amortization costs, of course. While capital amortization is treated as an input cost for each step of semiconductor production, the interest charge is handled as an overhead factor. All capital costs are simply totaled, and interest charges on the total are levied through successive periods of the simulation.

Unit Cost Calculations

Once the preliminary steps outlined above have been taken, the model is ready for its main calculation routine. Yield curves, adjusted input requirements, and capital amortization numbers are all in place. The model now goes through a massive array operation in which labor, land, plant, and material input requirements for all technologies are multiplied by appropriate prices for all countries and simulation periods. As previously mentioned, the model allows for expected changes in all input prices for all countries.

Once this array multiplication is completed, total production costs for each technology, country, and simulation period are calculated. These are divided by final die yield (calculated as the product of the four process-specific yields) for each technology, country, and simulation period. The result is a complete time profile of factory unit costs for all countries and technologies. Further calculations add interest charges and transport charges for non-US producers, on the assumption that sales in the US market are the object of production activity.

Once all these numbers have been generated, the model can identify the optimum technology for each country and the production sites whose relatively low unit costs identify them as potentially superior competitors in the DRAM market. At this point, the model also introduces the evolution of unit memory price, which is assumed to continue trending downward at its historical rate of approximately 40 percent annually. This unit price is translated to its capacity equivalent for the chip market being simulated. Unit price/cost ratios are then calculated for each simulation period using adjusted unit prices and the unit costs calculated by the model. The model is thus capable of generating an enormous set of competitive calculations for a particular DRAM market. It has been designed to accept an arbitrary number of technologies, countries (or firms), and time periods.

4 The Automobile Industry

In broad outline, the emerging dynamics in the world automotive industry look similar to those in electronics. Three features of the current competitive environment are particularly noteworthy. First, microelectronics are having a powerful impact on production technologies in the industrial countries. Possibilities for labor-saving mass production or flexible custom assembly are expanding rapidly. Secondly, product innovation continues at a rapid pace. Microelectronics and new materials are beginning to have a pronounced impact on automotive products. Some current models incorporate high-strength plastic body components and radically new transmission and steering systems. The next few years will witness replacement of metal by ceramics in major engine components; replacement of traditional wiring by single-cable communications systems linking smart power chips; and the advent of computer mapping and first-generation vehicle guidance systems.

Third, the world industry is rapidly evolving toward a new structure in the wake of Japan's meteoric rise, a reactive surge of automotive protectionism in the West, and unprecedented recent swings in currency values. Competition is becoming more pronounced at all quality levels; companies are searching for positions of comparative advantage in complex, interlocking international alliances. Much greater out-sourcing of components has been a prominent feature of the relentless pressure to cut costs. In some cases, the new locational economics are dictating the return of components production to automated facilities near assembly plants. Where automation remains too costly, new components suppliers in the NICs and developing countries are being offered unprecedented opportunities for market expansion.

In this chapter, we cannot hope to provide a full analysis of emerging developments in the world's biggest industry.[1] Our major focus will be on the new economics of motor vehicle assembly as practiced by incumbents (exemplified by US companies), innovators (Japanese firms), and new entrants (exemplified by Korean firms). We will pay particular attention to the future prospects of the

Koreans, who have become aggressive exporters. As independent producers or contract suppliers to·US firms, they have joined other NIC producers in the rush for North American market share.

The competitive success of Korea and the other NICs in this venture is far from assured. As in the case of garments, microelectronics raises the prospect of "de-maturing" in automobile production – a radical restructuring of the industry. The difference lies in the greater likelihood of such restructuring. US auto firms obviously have the money and the will to undertake it. Many of their products have remained sheltered from foreign competition by the North American preference for large cars. Substantial market power, low fuel prices, a rising Yen, and steady GNP growth in the US have combined to yield big profits in recent years. The Big Three have had the option of investing heavily in automation from internal funds and have chosen to do so.

It should also be noted that the US producers have been badly shaken by Japanese successes in the small and mid-size markets. With the rapid build-up of Japanese production capacity in the US, the domestic industry has realized substantial gains in quality and efficiency. Finally, the US auto producers are unlike many garment firms in the degree of their historic commitment to manufacturing itself. Aside from a recent move toward purchase of small import units to protect their entry-level market share, they have not shared many garment firms' apparent inclination to favor merchandising over domestic production.

The stage therefore seems to be set for a period of rapid technological change and intense competition in the North American auto market. As a prelude to the chapter, we offer the following thoughts on developments in the near future:

1. Korea as an exporter of assembled vehicles and major mechanical components will not experience significant competition from low-labor cost countries such as China and India. Among the newly-industrializing countries, only Brazil is somewhat plausible as a major competitor.

2. Microelectronics-induced automation, consumer product tailoring, and shortened response times have enhanced the prospect that US manufacturers can continue earning comfortable margins on larger vehicles during the next few years. Current joint production experience with Toyota in the NUMMI operation bodes well for compact auto production as well. Thus, the present move toward sourcing entry-level units from Korea and

elsewhere may be designed simply to buy time until newly-automated assembly operations come onstream.

3. Whether or not US firms become cost-competitive with new technology and restructuring, it is certain that Japanese firms are capable of producing compact units in North America at low cost. Thus, Korean prospects for profitable sales depend heavily on strategic decisions by the Japanese. At present, they are launching a new series of upscale products. It remains to be seen, however, whether they have any attention of ceding entry-level sales to the Koreans.

At present, Korea is enjoying competitive success in the US subcompact market. Both captive and direct sales strategies seem viable in the near future. As we have noted above, however, important questions remain to be answered. While Korea is engaged in intensive learning about technologies that are more or less "conventional", a new learning curve is emerging in North America. The major Japanese and American firms are all continuing massive investments in factory automation. Korea's fortunes as an auto exporter in the next decade will be heavily affected by the success of these investments.

KOREA'S CURRENT AUTO PRODUCTION PLANS

As in the case of semiconductors, the plans of the Korean majors in automobile production are quite ambitious. From the Korean perspective, there is nothing new in this. In the early 1970s, President Park Chung Hee termed auto production a "strategic export industry". The first serious attempts at production for export were launched late in the decade. Hyundai introduced the Pony in 1976, and production expanded steadily until 1979. Unfortunately, early export plans foundered on the recession induced by the second oil shock in 1979. By 1980, Korean auto producers were operating at only 24 percent of capacity, and the Korean government intervened to attempt a major restructuring of the industry.

At that time, the industry was composed of four firms: Hyundai, Saehan (ownership: 50 percent Daewoo, 50 percent General Motors), Kia, and Dong-A. The government wanted Hyundai to merge with Saehan, but the plan foundered when Hyundai insisted on dominating the merger. This dispute was symptomatic of a larger disagreement about Korean industrial development strategy. In the early 1980s, a consulting study (Hervey, 1982), described the historical strategy of the Korean government in the automotive sector as follows:

1. To build a largely independent group of vehicle manufacturers.
2. To require high and balanced local product content with no credits for exports of components and sub-assemblies.
3. To emphasize exports of finished vehicles.
4. To allow the relatively smaller component manufacturers to develop with less government assistance.

This was described as a "vehicle down" strategy, which would use the development of vehicles themselves as the engine of sectoral growth. It was contrasted with a possible "component up" export strategy, which would emphasize technology and marketing links with major auto producers in the OECD countries.

The Korean conglomerates have had differing views on the advisability of the two strategies. By far the most prominent exponent of the "vehicle down" strategy has been Hyundai, which redirected an early export drive for the Pony from the Third World towards Canada in late 1983. Hyundai's initial sales target for Canada was 5000 vehicles per year. Its introductory announcement excited no response from the established producers, since they regarded the 10-year-old Pony design as crude and unlikely to present any major challenge. They were wrong. In January 1986, Hyundai's Pony and Stellar models were selling at a rate equal to 10 percent of *total* Canadian auto demand (Keller, 1986). Since then, Hyundai has had unprecedented success with its introduction of the Excel in the US market. It planned to sell 100 000 units in the first year, but sold many more – a record number, in fact, for a first-year export. The company's goal for 1987 was 250 000 and it announced plans to export 400 000 units in 1988. At this point, the North American market seems to be speaking loudly in favor of the Korean producer. Hyundai intends to dampen protectionist sentiment in the US by installing at least some productive capacity onshore.

For the two other major Korean vehicle manufacturers, the captive route seems to be recommending itself at present. Daewoo intends to sell up to 100 000 units a year to GM's Pontiac division, and to have a production capacity of 278 000 units by 1988. Meanwhile, the Korean government has reversed its interventionist stand of the early 1980s. In 1985, it declared that in order to introduce an additional measure of competition, any existing vehicle manufacturer would be permitted to assemble the product of choice beginning in 1987.[2] This permitted Kia to begin supplying Ford with Mazda-designed subcompacts.

The present consensus among US industry observers and analysts is that Korea's prospects are bright in entry-level subcompact production. The 1986 predicition of one prominent analyst – that by 1990 Korean sales in the US would be around 500 000 units (Keller, 1986) – has looked quite good to many. As we noted previously, however, the consensus may well be wrong. Later in the chapter, we will present the results of our own analysis, with particular attention paid to the underlying dynamic issues and the quantitative results of our modeling exercise.

KOREA'S COMPETITIVE STATUS

Cheap, semi-skilled labor has never had as important a role in auto assembly as in semiconductor or garment production. The latter have historically involved "island" operations in which individual operators could come down learning curves with little organizational interaction. Auto assembly, on the other hand, has always been large, complex, and interactive. The major skills which must be mastered before competitive auto production can be undertaken are therefore not individual but organizational.[3]

Under these circumstances, Korea's strategic rear is much better covered in automobiles than in garments. China, for example, should pose no significant competitive threat in the near future. It should be noted that the Chinese are aware of their organizational shortcomings, and are actively discussing possibilities for massive technical assistance from outside. Chrysler recently signed an agreement to design and equip a plant with the capacity to produce 300 000 four-cylinder engines per year for First Automotive Works of Changchun, China's largest vehicle maker.[4] Active discussions have been held with General Motors and Honda about the possibility of building up a world-competitive auto industry from scratch. Clearly, however, such a program would be many years in the making. Although GM has stepped up its involvement with China, GM's Director of Program Planning for China, Stephen Chen, has been quoted as stating: "I cannot see any possibility this century for external development of the Chinese automobile industry."[5]

The same thing seems to hold true for producers in other countries with extremely low labor costs, such as India. Although India has been producing vehicles for a long time, Indian producers have shown little significant movement on the learning curve and are far from international competitiveness at present in most motor vehicle categories.

Thus Korea's only near-term competitors at the entry level seem to be the established OECD producers and several aspiring firms in the newly-industrializing countries. The most notable of these at present are in Yugoslavia, Mexico, Taiwan, Malaysia and Brazil. Yugoslavia's first offspring, the Yugo, has been plagued by a bad safety and quality image; its prospects remain highly uncertain. The Mexican domestic assembly industry has been plagued by low volumes, and Mexican competitiveness to date has been in production of labor-intensive components such as wire harnesses. Plans for the sale of assembled vehicles in the US may suffer from the dominance of US and European multinationals which are themselves trying to "relearn the trade" by adopting Japanese organizational techniques.[6]

Malaysia hopes to break into the American market with the Saga, a modification of the Mitsubishi Lancer Fiore. This vehicle is assembled by Proton, a national firm which has been touted as the flagship of President Mahathir's heavy industrialization strategy. At present, Malaysian content is limited to tires, batteries, seat cushions, and some minor trimmings. Efficiency is low, and industry analysts believe that competitive pricing in the North American market would require heavy state subsidies for a long time. Although Bricklin Industries has announced plans to import 100 000 Sagas in 1988, rising to 250 000 units in 5 years, it is not clear that the Malaysian government would be able to sustain the heavy financial losses associated with competitive pricing. The agreement with Bricklin calls for Mitsui to sponsor a major migration of international component manufacturers into Malaysia to support the industry, but the whole enterprise is still highly problematic. There is currently no evidence that Proton will move down the learning curve fast enough for profitability in US competition with the Korean firms.

Korea's major NIC competitor in Asia, Taiwan, has also entered the auto market. The two countries share certain disadvantages: a limited domestic market; relatively undeveloped design/engineering capabilities; the lack of a sophisticated components industry. However, Korea has the advantage afforded by a larger, more sophisticated heavy industrial manufacturing base. While technology/

component multisourcing by Taiwan (through Nissan and Ford) is an essential feature of its short/medium-term strategy, Korea's producers seem more capable of establishing vertically-integrated, efficient automobile production *systems* as opposed to components assembly operations. Since current trends suggest a declining importance for low-cost labor in any case, it is the existence of such efficient systems which will probably form part of a successful competitive strategy.

Thus, among current Asian aspirants, Korea seems best positioned for success in automotive production. Against competition from Brazil, whose technical/industrial base is well-established, Korea's prospects are more uncertain. Brazil may be poised to play a major role at the low end of the North American market, with modernized Volkswagen models whose development costs have long since been amortized. Brazilian wages are not significantly above those in Korea, and Brazil has been assembling automobiles for a long time. During the past few years, Brazil has demonstrated considerable success in exporting high-quality light aircraft and light military vehicles. Korea may therefore find it to be a formidable competitor.

At present, however, the Brazilian industry seems to be in difficulty. The major players, Ford and Volkswagen, have both seen their plans disrupted by lower-than-expected growth of the Brazilian economy. They have recently merged all their Brazilian and Argentinian operations into a composite company, Autolina. Brazil imposes stringent domestic content requirements (90 percent), so that Autolina cannot be integrated into an efficient international production system.[7] Thus, the prospects for Brazilian competitiveness in the short-intermediate term do not seem overwhelmingly bright.

Among the NICs Korea seems to stand the best chance of becoming a major international player. In relation to the OECD producers, however, Korea's potential disadvantages are numerous and obvious. What are the prospects, then, for Korean producers to compete against established OECD firms at *any* level of the market, including subcompact production?

Korea's major advantage is its well-educated, motivated, and relatively low-cost labor force at both the operational and technical levels.[8] In addition, the Korean conglomerates can use profits from other product lines to finance large investments in physical and technical capacity for automobile research, design, and production. Korean firms have made a commitment to auto production, and they are unquestionably coming down the industry learning curve at a considerable speed.[9] Against them the OECD producers have arrayed: decades of production experience; tremendously long production runs, particularly for large domestic markets; great depth in engineering and design capabilities; immediate proximity to and intimate knowledge of domestic markets. In addition, of course, they now have the benefits of recent developments in microelectronics.

A basic question therefore remains unanswered. Does Korea's initial success in the North American auto market have solid long-term foundations, or is it the result of a temporary conjunction of forces which will diverge again in the near future? For now, the Yen is high and US assemblers need low-cost non-Japanese subcompact suppliers while they build highly automated assembly plants. In a few years, however, market conditions may change drastically.

THE NORTH AMERICAN MARKET FOR SMALL CARS

Potential Competition from US Firms

The conventional wisdom among industry experts has been that US automakers will not attempt cost-competitive production of small cars during the rest of the decade. In their view GM, Ford and Chrysler will attempt to control the "beachhead" by importing units from Japan, Korea, and elsewhere. (Salter *et al.*, 1985). This consensus, while it may be correct, is nothing more than an extrapolation from past experience. It is clear that the US producers are already concentrated in the mid-size and large segments of the auto market. Table 4.1 provides a view of intended product introductions for the balance of the decade as of 1986.

These numbers do leave an impression of a retreat by domestic auto manufacturers to the mid- and large-size segments of the market. It should be noted, however, that the relatively few offerings anticipated from domestic manufacturers will be produced in very considerable numbers. The major new US entries in the small car market will be the GM Saturn (250 000–500 000/year) and the Chrysler P-Body (300 000/year).

Competitive strategy will center on relatively few basic products, produced in huge automated complexes, which will be differentiated through options to suit different consumer tastes.

It remains to be seen whether the continuation of low oil prices will have a major impact on the structure of demand in North America.

TABLE 4.1   *Summary of new product introductions and announcements in the US market by American, Japanese, and Korean automakers*

	1980–85	1986–90	Total
Small			
Domestic	3	2	5
Korean/Japanese	22	8	30
Mid-size			
Domestic	5	4	9
Korean/Japanese	15	2	17
Large Luxury			
Domestic	8	4	12
Korean/Japanese	0	0	0

SOURCE: Salter *et al.* (1986).

Consumer tastes have undoubtedly changed since the first oil shock, and it seems unlikely that the distribution of demand by automobile size class will return to its former pattern. Nevertheless, it is of interest to note the profound change between 1973 and 1982 (Table 4.2).

With the continued low level of oil prices, demand has been shifting back toward the 1973 distribution. In response, General Motors and other producers have been steadily adjusting the size distribution of their auto offerings.[10]

For Korean producers, the fall in oil prices has had mixed implications. Their own fuel cost has fallen substantially, but there is at least the possibility that the demand for small automobiles in the United States will decline even faster. This development would obviously play to the strength of US firms.

Are these firms capable of competing with the Koreans at the low end of the market? Under the old rules of the game, the answer to this question was clearly negative. Indeed, the conventional wisdom among industry analysts has been that the domestic manufacturers are unlikely to return to competitiveness at the low end of the market. Three reasons are generally cited:

1. Labor is simply too expensive and inefficient, whatever labor-saving technologies or structural reforms are adopted.
2. Management is so mired in outmoded structures that it will never be able to adapt effectively.
3. Designers no longer understand consumer tastes.

TABLE 4.2 *US market shares by vehicle size, 1973 and 1982*

		1973	1982
Very Large		57	30
Large		20	26
Medium		15	17
Light		6	23
Small		2	4

Definitions:	*Small*	*Light*	*Medium*	*Large*	*V. Large*
Engine size (cc)	up to 1200	1200–1400	1400–1800	1800–2600	2600 +
Wheelbase (in)	up to 92	92–98	98–102	102–108	108 +
Weight (lb)	up to 1750	1750–2000	2000–2400	2400–3000	3000 +

SOURCE: Roos, Altshuler *et al.* (1984).

Extreme proponents of these views believe that it is only a matter of time before the US auto market is completely dominated by the Japanese, Koreans, and others. They think that the Japanese in particular are constrained only by their sensitivity to protectionist sentiments in the US and the speed with which they can install capacity in North America. A corollary view is that Hyundai, which has no previous experience with the management of resources and markets in North America, can do better than GM, Ford and Chrysler simply because it is starting fresh.

These are, of course, only opinions. Time will tell whether the US manufacturers are capable of adapting with sufficient speed to overcome the current Japanese and Korean cost advantage. For the present, we will confine outselves to hard evidence on intentions and potential capabilities. Our modeling exercise will attempt to incorporate current expert opinion about what is possible with known and emerging technologies. As to the three points cited above, we might offer the following observations.

The argument that US labor is uncompetitive has been effectively disproven by the Japanese. Honda and Nissan have maintained a very healthy cost advantage at their North American plants. At NUMMI, GM has made the "startling" discovery that under the Toyota production system, a low-cost medium technology operation can still be very productive. It is shuttling as many personnel as possible through NUMMI, and the other US producers are beginning to bid for managers and workers who have been trained in the Japanese production system at US plants.

In our interviews with auto industry people, we have found no evidence of a refusal to accept Japanese production and management innovations. Managers of current leapfrogging projects, such as Saturn, already know that cost-competitive small cars can be built by North American workers without technological leaps. Even in their conventional operations, the domestic producers are moving quickly. According to a recent press report, GM's newly modernized assembly plant in Linden, N.J. requires just 29 employee hours to build each Corsica and Beretta compact. This represents a drastic improvement on the 40 hours required at less advanced GM plants, although it still lags the 23-hour average at NUMMI. By all accounts, quality has also improved substantially.[11]

The argument that US producers have lost their feel for appealing designs seems wrong in light of recent evidence. Chrysler's innovative minivan has appealed strongly to "baby boom" families; it dominates a competing Toyota product in a market where Japanese imports are not constrained. Ford's mid-size offering, the Taurus, is a response to consumer interest in European styling. After the product was introduced in December, 1985, there were immediate orders for 115 000 units – four times the expected volume and one quarter of the year's planned production.[12] General Motors' innovative Pontiac Fiero, a small European-style sports car fabricated from high-strength plastics, has been in a permanent state of excess demand because GM has chosen to produce only 100 000 units per year. The design argument simply does not seem to hold water.

But does it make economic sense for US firms to compete with the Koreans and others at the entry level? There are two schools of thought about the economic rationale. One view stresses static optimality, while the other has a dynamic perspective. Consideration only of the current account would certainly dictate that US firms concentrate on the luxury and full-size portions of the market. Automobiles in this range are strongly differentiated products, and consumer demand for their luxury features is relatively inelastic. Substantially greater net revenues per sale are therefore possible.

However, a strategy focused solely on upscale models ignores another feature of the automobile market which differentiates it strongly from the markets for garments and semiconductors. All three goods have more than one characteristic (e.g. quality, reliability) which is valued by customers, but automobiles represent extremely complex packages whose expense (even at the "low end") is sufficiently great for consumers to view them as long-term investments. Purchasing an automobile is a complex, time-consuming task. US consumers are therefore prone to regard their initial foray into the auto market as an investment in a dealer relationship. If they are satisfied with their initial choice, they tend to return if the dealer has produced offerings which match their rising incomes and aspirations.

US producers have always been aware of this, of course, but they were caught off guard by the sudden shift in the structure of US demand during the 1970s as the post-war baby boom generation came of age simultaneously with the first oil shock. GM has recently undergone a major internal restructuring which suggests very strongly that it is committed to product offerings aimed at capturing consumers as they enter the auto market for the first time. Chrysler and Ford are clearly committed to low-end offerings, even if Ford seem to have opted for captive imports.

We conclude that the domestic producers look quite resilient at this point. In balance, it would undoubtedly be a mistake for aspiring auto producers in Korea and elsewhere to assume that their entry into US markets cannot or will not be contested by domestic manufacturers.

Potential Competition from Japanese Firms

The Japanese are currently developing a fully-diversified product line in the US. Recently, they have begun introducing a series of mid-size models for sale in upscale markets. Honda introduced its high-priced Acura line in March 1986, to general critical and consumer acclaim. Honda expected sales of 110 000 units in 1987, with more than double that number by 1990.[13] Nissan and Toyota introduced luxury models, the Infiniti and Lexus, respectively, in 1989.

Their own success has made the Japanese firms wary of the Korean beachhead strategy.[14] They are very unlikely to cede the low end of the market without a struggle. As we will show in our own cost analysis, their compact offerings are priced well above the unit cost of production in their US factories. A strong price-cutting response to a Korean challenge would undermine any Korean hope for profitable auto exports in the short run.

It should not be imagined that such a response is implausible. This is exactly what happened in the 256K DRAM market in the face of a downturn in chip demand in 1985. The Japanese response was price-cutting so severe that all the Korean majors and most US producers were forced out of the market. The US producers have political means of protection, as evidenced by the recent rash of dumping suits against Japanese semiconductor firms launched by the US Government. Korean producers, of course, have few political defenses. If they compete by taking short-run losses, they are nearly as vulnerable as the Japanese to dumping charges. Because the US producers' general market position would not be affected in the same way, current captive arrangements between GM-Daewoo and Ford-Kia would probably not be affected as severely. On balance, then, recent events have shifted the long-run betting odds at least slightly in the direction of the GM-Daewoo strategy.

SOURCES OF JAPAN'S CURRENT ADVANTAGE

The Japanese enjoy their current cost advantage over all rivals for three main reasons:[15] (1) superior learning; (2) automation; and (3) economies of scale. The Japanese advantage over US producers is primarily due to superior learning, while their advantage over the Koreans and other NIC producers stems from all three factors. The Japanese advantage over Korea in economies of scale is, of course, immutable in the short run. It is, however, balanced to a considerable degree by the Korean advantage in wages. The current economics of production are summarized in Table 4.3, which compares unit costs for a complex vehicle component produced under typical operating conditions in the US, Japan and Korea. The Korean advantage is obviously overwhelming in one area: Extremely long working hours and low pay. In Table 4.3, for example, Japanese hourly labor costs are $23, as opposed to $4 in Korea. Japanese working hours (1960/year) are also substantially below those of Korean workers (2400/year).

The Japanese advantages, however, more than compensate for the difference in hours and earnings. It can probably be argued that Japan has moved down the learning curve in automobile production more effectively than any other nation. At present, Japanese superiority shows most crucially in four numbers:

1. *Direct labor productivity*: The major Japanese assemblers are world leaders in the application of human skills to production tasks, and the work force in Japanese auto plants is distingu-

TABLE 4.3 *Illustrative comparative unit cost exercise complex cast/forged-and-machined auto subassembly*

Production:	500 000 units/year	
US Assumptions:	2 hours per unit direct labor	
	Indirect-to-direct labor ratio:	1:1
	Direct material per unit:	$150
	Hours per worker per year:	1880
	Equipment amortization:	$50 per unit
	Work-in-process cost:	$10 per unit

	International Comparisons	
	Japan	Korea
Hourly labor cost	$23	$4
Direct labor productivity*	120	50
Indirect: direct ratio	.6:1	.8:1
Hours worked per year	1960	2400
Machine utilization	85%	60%
Materials cost index*	100	95
Scrap factor	2%	20%
WIP cost	$5	$15

* Relative to U.S. equivalent

	Current Relative Production Costs	
	Japan	Korea
Direct and indirect labor	$68.74	$28.60
Direct material	145.71	162.86
Equipment amortization	58.82	83.33
Transportation, tariff	20.00	20.00
WIP cost	5.00	15.00
Total	293.27	294.79

SOURCE: Dan Luria, Industrial Technology Institute (adapted for recent changes in exchange rates and wages)

ished by high levels of education, flexibility and motivation. In the illustration, this translates to a labor productivity ratio of 2.4:1 when Korean workers are used as the basis for comparison.

2. *Machine utilization*: Japanese machine utilization rates are estimated to be higher than those in Korea. Again, this is symptomatic of the degree to which effective learning over a number of years in Japan has maximized "time on task" in production operations.

3. *Indirect: direct labor ratio*: The Japanese advantage in this category stems both from economies of scale and from learning over a long period of time about the organization of auto production. In this estimate, the Korean ratio is 33 percent greater than the Japanese ratio.

4. *Scrap factor*: The scrap factor ratio in this estimate is 10:1 and is clearly an important source of the overall cost differential between Korea and Japan. In part, this factor is due to superior Japanese automation and manufacturing precision. Part is due, as well, to superior learning because of more extensive production experience.

When these numbers are translated to unit costs, Japanese competitiveness becomes strikingly apparent. Even at the current inflated value of the Yen, Japanese unit costs are slightly lower than Korean costs.

Thus, the current production frontier is clearly defined by the Japanese vehicle production system.[16] Given current technology, Japanese producers are probably near the efficiency limit in auto production.[17] Korean producers, on the other hand, are just starting down the learning curve. *Given current technology*, it could be expected that Korea would assume world cost leadership in small car production. This can readily be seen by simply attributing Japan's current unit costs for material, equipment amortization, and work-in-process to Korea. Even with substantial Korean wage growth in the interim, the numbers would look overwhelmingly favorable for Korea.

EMERGING TECHNOLOGIES: THE POSSIBILITY OF "DE-MATURING"

Unfortunately for Korea and other NICs, the auto production frontier will not remain stable. US producers (particularly General Motors) plan to move the frontier quite rapidly in the near future through the application of CIM (computer-integrated manufacturing), CAD (computer-aided design) and computer-enhanced product marketing. Thus, the problem of Korea's auto producers during the coming half-decade may be similar (although somewhat less urgent, given the difference in product cycles) to the problem of semiconductor manufacturers. While Korean auto producers are moving down the learning curve towards a low-cost limit defined by standard technology, US producers are midway through a massive program to build highly automated production facilities. In the meantime, the Japanese will certainly continue with incremental improvements and may move rapidly towards automation themselves.

Prospects for a Technological Leap by US Producers

The US automobile industry is experiencing a period of rapid change, in which the historical pattern of incrementalism has been replaced by the explicit choice of high-risk, potentially high-return investment in advanced technology. In an interview, G. Frederic Bolling, Director of Ford's Manufacturing Development Center, distinguished three approaches to enhanced competitiveness:

1. *Extension*: Incremental improvements on existing practice, with concentration on micro-adjustments in existing facilities. This has been the practice in much of the US auto industry in the past, and the Japanese have proven themselves masters of the art.

2. *Leapfrogging*: The adoption of frontier technology in the attempt to jump past the productivity of a competitor, who may have learned more effectively about a past "best practice" technology. Current ambitious plans for factory automation fall into this category. Leapfrogging may generate considerable tension between engineering and financial control staffs within a firm, because it involves a substantial degree of risk and established accounting procedures do not take the associated benefits of generalized learning into account. Nevertheless, leapfrogging is a venture into the known in the sense that the engineers are undertaking something which they know is technically feasible. The problem, of course, is to derive correct estimates of the ultimate costs and benefits.

3. *Radical Change*: The adoption of approaches to automobile production which are not in any sense extensions of current practice. For obvious reasons, the US automobile companies are reluctant to talk about ideas in this category which they may be exploring. In the general climate of gossip floating around Detroit, however, one hears references to temporary factories housed in inflatable structures, production structures with all quality control built into the machinery, etc.

Given ample financial resources, it would seem logical for a major automobile producer to explore all three avenues for the enhance-

ment of competitive advantage. General Motors is the best positioned to undertake a diversity of experiments:[18] in the Extension
category, it has undertaken joint production with Toyota in a
consortium – New United Motor Manufacturing, Inc. (NUMMI).
Toyota has co-purchased a former GM production facility in Fremont, California, and NUMMI is producing Toyota Corolla designs
in the US market for Chevrolet under the Nova brand name. GM's
avowed goal for this venture is to learn the Toyota production system
first hand and to see which parts of it can easily be transferred to its
North American operations.

In the Leapfrog category, GM is busily engaged in installing
advanced factory automation systems throughout its system. Possibly
most significant is GM's new Saturn Corporation, which will manufacture compact automobiles in an automated complex in Tennessee
starting in 1990. GM's technology strategy has also motivated the
purchase of two large corporations outright – Electronic Data
Systems (EDS), which specializes in the establishment of large data
processing and electronic accounting systems; and Hughes Aircraft,
which has been one of the premier suppliers of high technology
electronics and aerospace products to the US Defense Department.
Both EDS and Hughes are now intimately involved in the integration
of microelectronics into General Motors' planning, product design,
marketing, and production.

GM has said almost nothing publicly about its operations in the
Radical Change category. It is known to be sponsoring several
projects aimed at fundamental rethinking of the automobile *product*
as well as the process, with emphasis on the incorporation of
advanced electronics, ceramics, and plastics. The use of plastics in the
highly-successful Pontiac Fiero suggests one tack in GM's current
thinking. Another is indicated by the Trilby project, which involves
enlistment of Hughes Aircraft for a complete redesign of automotive
control systems. Given Hughes' manifest ability to design, build, and
control most of the ultra-high resolution surveillance satellites of the
US Defense Department, there is certainly reason to suppose that it
can radically improve automobile electronics.

While GM has the resources to support three large exploratory
projects at once, Ford and Chrysler are more constrained. Both Ford
and Chrysler have undertaken heavy investments in automation, but
there is no evidence that Ford intends to put major resources into a
gamble on domestic production of small automobiles. Chrysler's

current plans do suggest a commitment to producing at least one more compact car generation (The P-Body series) in the US.

Will these US technology initiatives provide effective competition for entry-level offerings by Korea and other NICs? Many analysts have asserted that none of Detroit's offerings will offer meaningful competition for Korea's first generation auto exports.[19] This opinion is not shared by all, however, and GM is not tipping its hand publicly. It should be pointed out that the original genesis of the Saturn Project was precisely the realization that GM couldn't use existing production methods to produce a compact car competitive with Japanese models.[20]

One analysis of the US auto industry (Salter *et al.*, 1985) notes that Project Saturn was set up as a "clean sheet" systems approach to building a small car. No original deadline was imposed. Rather, the Saturn group was given the challenge of determining how to build small cars in the US by applying new technologies to product development and manufacturing. The product was to be both cost-competitive with small imported autos and clearly superior in terms of quality, safety, and performance.

At present, the major US firms are sinking enormous capital and intellectual resources into leapfrogging operations for the next decade. Their level of self-confidence is quite high, if our own interviews provide any guide. According to G. Frederic Bolling, any current Japanese or Korean advantage will be short-lived because US firms are simply going to get most of the labor content out of auto production. By the early 1990s, he foresees the opening of plants which are almost entirely automated. By 2000, he thinks that unmanned facilities will be commonplace. When he was asked recently about the potentional competitiveness of GM's design-phase electronic car, GM's President Roger Smith responded:

> I don't think that it's going to be "highly competitive" because I think we're going to own the technology. I believe it. I think we're really going to handle it. That's what we're starting out to do. There are going to be a lot of people that are going to have to play catch up. If we do this right we're going to be licensing a lot of people to use our technology.

As one industry analyst has pointed out, the Saturn Corporation cannot really be seen as a stand-alone operation, because GM intends to use it as a vehicle for starting its descent along an entirely new learning curve associated with full computer-integrated manufacturing. In the following section, we will introduce the major technologies which will define the new learning path.

New Technologies in Auto Manufacturing

As we noted previously, GM has made a major commitment to factory automation, emphasizing computer-aided design and manufacturing (CAD/CAM), robotics, and plant-floor communications. One key component in GM's strategy is its use of market power to impose a new industry standard computer communications protocol, introduced as MAP (Manufacturing Automation Protocol) in 1982. Large producers of computer equipment such as IBM and Digital Equipment Corporation are now designing MAP systems, and GM's equipment suppliers are all adapting their robotic and numerically-controlled systems to the MAP standard. The rapid emergence of this standard may well be the key to cost-effective implementation of GM's long-term strategy.

For implementing hardware advances, GM's strategy can best be depicted by outlining the new technologies which have recently been introduced.

1. *Hamtramck Assembly Plant*: Production in 1985; ultimate capacity 60 vehicles per hour in two shifts (approximately 240 000 vehicles per year); 5000 workers. Automation aspects:

   250 robots (160 in the body shop; 70 in the paint shop; 20 in general assembly).

   60 automated guided vehicles, which replace human fork lift operators in transporting materials to the assembly line.

   Modular body assembly – temporary attachment of underbody, side frames, and roof panel by operators; complete welding at one automated station.

   Robotic installation of doors, with machine vision alignment.

   Machine vision inspection of car bodies for adherence to fit and finish specifications.

Robotic application of sealants and paints.

Preliminary implementation of MAP.

2. *Saginaw Steering Gear Plant*: Fabrication of front-wheel drive axles; startup in early 1986:

Phase One: Integration of the plant's 40 manufacturing cells with MAP.

Phase Two (1987): Complete integration of the manufacturing cells with the central factory control system. Debut of the "paperless factory", with automated product changeovers, instruction downloading, and work verification.

3. *Saturn*: Assembly of a new compact vehicle; automated assembly complex opening in 1990.

Because Saturn involves a whole new approach to manufacturing, its main aspects will be discussed here in some detail.

Vehicle design, manufacturability

Two major innovations are being planned by the Saturn Project. First, great emphasis will be placed on modular assemblies as a way of enhancing quality and balancing the work load in final assembly. The modules (for example engines, transmissions, instruments, seats, doors) are expected to be built in areas near the assembly line. Flexible techniques and reprogrammable robots are expected to permit the assembly of a wide array of body styles on the same line, albeit at somewhat slower rates than current lines. Changeovers to new models should proceed much more quickly than current practice allows. The present plan is to use automatically guided vehicles for all phases of transport, including the assembly line itself. At this point, the moving assembly line will be a thing of the past, and workers will be able to ensure quality installation before a vehicle is despatched to the next station.

Parts sourcing

The exact percentage of Saturn's component parts which will be produced on-site is not yet clear, but a good estimate is that GM's historic out-sourcing percentage of 35–45 per cent will increase to around 65 per cent with Saturn. Domestic parts suppliers whose workers are not in the United Auto Workers Union generally have labor costs about half those of the assemblers themselves. Many parts are available from foreign suppliers (particularly in East Asia) at lower unit costs, although GM's adoption of "just-in-time" inventory techniques seems to preclude major dependence on overseas sources. Rather, the preferred arrangement will probably be domestic automated production at satellite plants of the Saturn complex. [21]

Some of the independently owned suppliers may actually operate in space leased from Saturn in the building housing final assembly. This would allow for synchronized delivery of major modules. At present, the only components that seem sure to be produced by Saturn (or a GM division at the Saturn site) are the engine, automatic transmission/manual gear boxes, major stampings, and a few large plastic mouldings.

Castings

North American engine components have traditionally been produced with ferrous metals using sand casting technology. By contrast, Saturn will have an aluminium engine block and head which will be cast in near-final form by the "lost foam" technique. This approach uses a coated (perishable) polystyrene pattern/core, which allows engineers to design much more complex castings. It is currently thought that full application of this technique will reduce Saturn engine block and head machining time by a third.

Materials

By contemporary standards, Saturn will be an extremely light vehicle. While GM "J" cars such as the Chevrolet Cavalier weigh 2750 pounds, the Saturn's projected weight is 2125 pounds. It may be even lighter, if GM can overcome current limitations on industry capacity for mass provision of plastic body panels. Saturn's major weight-saving contributors will be aluminium castings, an aluminium rather than copper radiator, increased use of high-strength galvanized steel, further penetration of plastics, and a new lighter transmission.

Marketing

The goal of full electronic integration for Saturn extends beyond factory-level integration through MAP. Through its EDS subsidiary, GM is designing a coordination system which will allow vehicle marketing and delivery to be electronically integrated as well. Under the current plan, buyers would be able to choose color and optional equipment, arrange for credit and financing, and get a delivery date, all from a computer terminal at a dealership or (the aspiration of some marketing radicals) from mini-dealerships at shopping malls. Customer orders would be converted automatically into parts orders, and all relevant components would begin flowing through the delivery system at the appropriate pace for simultaneous arrival at the final assembly point. The current hope is to compress the cycle from consumer order to delivery to 12 days.

FUTURE PRODUCTION COSTS

In the previous section, we have discussed the flow of new technologies which the US manufacturers, particularly GM, intend to bring onstream during the next half decade in an attempt to leapfrog Japanese and Korean producers. In this section we use our dynamic costing model, auto technology vectors produced by our own research, and present and anticipated input prices to explore the prospects of Korea's auto producers in the North American auto market during the coming decade. A detailed description of the technology vectors and input price data can be found in the Appendix to this chapter. Our modeling approach for autos is similar to that for semiconductors in the sense that we assume vertically-integrated production operations within each competitor country. Three countries are considered: Korea, the US and Japan. As before, three technologies (Manual, Semi-Automated, and Robotic) are specified, and resulting unit costs are calculated using data on local conditions and input costs. For Robotic technology, we have assumed start-up in 1988 in both Japan and the US. We would expect production to remain well below final capacity for a good while, as the Robotic operations begin coming down a new learning curve. By the early 1990s they should be well down the curve.

Table 4.4 below portrays a representative set of results, which are produced using the technology and input price data specified in

Table 4.4 *Projected unit costs for compact auto production 1987–97*

Year	Manual (Korea)	Semi-automated Korea	Semi-automated US	Semi-automated Japan	Robotic[1] US	Robotic[1] Japan	Robotic[2] US	Robotic[2] Japan
1987	2435	2477	2889	3058	–	–	–	–
1988	2449	2465	2931	3098	2836	2936	3374	3465
1989	2463	2461	2976	3140	2660	2739	3096	3169
1990	2478	2461	3023	3184	2577	2646	2961	3025
1991	2493	2464	3073	3229	2542	2606	2901	2959
1992	2510	2470	3125	3276	2534	2593	2879	2934
1993	2527	2478	3179	3326	2538	2595	2877	2930
1994	2545	2486	3237	3377	2550	2605	2886	2936
1995	2564	2496	3297	3430	2566	2619	2900	2948
1996	2583	2507	3360	3485	2585	2636	2918	2964
1997	2604	2519	3426	3543	2606	2654	2939	2982

Unit cost for least-cost production technology, 1987–97[3]

	Korea Cost	Korea Tech.	US Cost	US Tech.	Japan Cost	Japan Tech.
1987	2435	1	2889	2	3058	2
1988	2449	1	2931	2	3098	2
1989	2461	2	2976	2	3140	2
1990	2461	2	2961	3	3025	3
1991	2464	2	2901	3	2959	3
1992	2470	2	2879	3	2934	3
1993	2478	2	2877	3	2930	3
1994	2486	2	2886	3	2936	3
1995	2496	2	2900	3	2948	3
1996	2507	2	2918	3	2964	3
1997	2519	2	2939	3	2982	3

[1] Corresponds to $1 billion investment in Robotic plant.
[2] Corresponds to $2 billion investment in Robotic plant.
[3] For the technologies, Manual = 1; Semi-Automated = 2; Robotic = 3. For the US and Japan, a $2 billion Robotic investment is assumed.

Appendix 4.[22] It provides some insight into the probable future of competition in the North American compact automobile market. The first column depicts unit costs for Manual production technology in Korea from 1987 to 1997. Korean producers continue down the learning curve at a rapid pace, but increased efficiency is balanced by rapidly-rising Korean wages.

The next three columns forecast unit costs for Semi-Automated technology in Korea, the US and Japan. The US column provides a forecast of unit production costs in North America with technology currently employed by Toyota, Nissan, Honda, and other Japanese firms. Since this technology is mature, residual learning curve movement is not sufficient to overcome the impact of continuing wage inflation. Costs rise in consequence through 1997.

In Japan, the unit cost with Semi-Automated technology also rises as wage inflation overcomes diminishing returns to learning. Since Semi-Automated technology is currently operating in both North America and Japan, these numbers provide a framework within which the current competitive status of Korean producers can be assessed. Two additional factors have to be considered before a consideration of true comparative cost in the US market can be undertaken. First, technology license fees are an important factor for the Koreans. The Hyundai Excel, for example, is produced under agreements with Mitsubishi which involve a fee of approximately 15 percent of the purchase price. Since the lowest-priced Excel has recently sold for $4995 in the US, the implied license fee is $750. The full cost of transportation from Korea and Japan to the US can be estimated at $500. Therefore, $1250 and $500 are added to the unit cost of automobiles shipped from Korea and Japan for simulated comparison with US-produced units. The results are portrayed in Table 4.5.

Korean autos sold in the US are currently less costly than their US or Japanese counterparts produced by Semi-Automated technology, and their advantage increases in the 1990s. Korean producers continue down the learning curve, while mature technologies in the US and Japan cannot support enough additional learning to overcome input price inflation. By 1995, Korean autos are least-cost if license fees are assumed to be terminated.

Finally, we consider the possibility of Robotic production in the US and Japan under two assumptions. Estimated US market costs for $1 billion and $2 billion Robotic investments are presented in the last four columns of Table 4.5. On the assumption that a viable automated plant of the type depicted in Table A.4.1 (in Appendix 4) can start down the learning curve by 1988, and that such a plant costs $1 billion, Korea's competitive prospects become dimmer. Under continued license fee payment, Korean landed costs are actually above those characterizing both US and Japanese Robotic production. By 1995, US Robotic production has unit costs more than $1100 below those of Korean imports. Robotically-produced Japanese imports are also lower than Korean imports in cost. However, if we change the

TABLE 4.5 *Projected costs for compact autos, US market 1987–97*

Year	Manual		Semi-automated				Robotic[1]		Robotic[2]	
	Korea[a]	Korea[b]	Korea[a]	Korea[b]	US	Japan[a]	US	Japan[a]	US	Japan[a]
1987	3685	2935	3727	2977	2889	3558	–	–	–	–
1988	3699	2949	3715	2965	2931	3598	2836	3436	3374	3965
1989	3713	2963	3711	2961	2976	3640	2660	3239	3096	3669
1990	3728	2978	3711	2961	3023	3684	2577	3146	2961	3525
1991	3743	2993	3714	2964	3073	3729	2542	3106	2901	3459
1992	3760	3010	3720	2970	3125	3776	2534	3093	2879	3434
1993	3777	3027	3728	2978	3179	3826	2538	3095	2877	3430
1994	3795	3045	3736	2986	3237	3877	2550	3105	2886	3436
1995	3814	3064	3746	2996	3297	3930	2566	3119	2900	3448
1996	3833	3083	3757	3007	3360	3985	2585	3136	2918	3464
1997	3854	3104	3769	3019	3426	4043	2606	3154	2939	3482

[a] Includes $1250 (license fee + landing cost) for Korea and $500 (landing cost) for Japan.
[b] Includes $500 (landing cost) for Korea.
[1] Corresponds to $1 billion investment in Robotic plant.
[2] Corresponds to $2 billion investment in Robotic plant.

assumed cost of a Robotic plant to $2 billion and assume suspension of license fees, Korea's prospects improve. In the mid-1990s, US Robotic production arrives at a unit cost almost identical to that of Korean imports. Japanese Robotic production appears less competitive.

Thus, our estimates suggest that Korean automobiles are likely to remain in the competitive cost range in the US market, even if Robotic production is undertaken. Any optimism produced by these results should be tempered, however, by a fundamental point. As we noted previously, entry-level competition is now considered strategic by all major players in the auto market.

Thus, it seems clear that the competitive environment for Korea is going to be much tougher than it was for Japan a decade ago. During the next few years, Japanese transplant production of compact autos is going to reach enormous volume in the US; producers themselves will have to move rapidly toward transplant unit cost levels if they are to survive as compact auto producers. Korean producers will not enter North America with the kind of $2000 cost advantage claimed for the Japanese around 1980. Whether they sell directly (as Hyundai has chosen to do) or using captive arrangements (the chosen route of Daewoo and Kia), they will at best have a small cost advantage over domestically-produced units. If the Korean majors choose to produce in the US themselves, there is no reason to suppose that they will operate plants which are more cost-effective than those of Toyota or Honda.

Our Robotic numbers suggest that even if US producers do not become efficient enough to continue producing compact autos, the Japanese may see the compelling rationale for automating their US operations. We conclude that Korea's North American auto venture is potentially a success, but carries substantial risks. Our analysis suggests that Hyundai will be operating with very low profit margins for a number of years if it chooses to compete for a substantial share of the North American market. Since our results indicate that all viable producers will have production costs substantially below Hyundai's current selling price, the possibility of a damaging price war cannot be ruled out.

APPENDIX 4: MODELING COMPETITIVE COST DYNAMICS IN COMPACT AUTOMOBILE PRODUCTION

Our work on automobiles has proceeded in a manner similar to the modeling exercises for semiconductors, textiles, and garments. We began with a review of existing quantitative models and forecasts pertaining to compact automobile production. Once we understood the basic processes involved and the existing consensus about the future evolution of production, we undertook an extensive round of interviews in the Japanese automobile industry. Thanks to the intervention of several highly-placed Japanese scholars and industry consultants, we were able to arrange interviews with top technical and managerial people at Toyota and Nissan.[23]

Since our return from Japan, we have consulted extensively with auto industry experts in universities, consulting firms, and the major US automobile firms. Our interviews in the US provided us with access to much new published and unpublished work on the future of technology and auto competition, as well as first-hand information about emerging developments. Finally, our collaborator Dr Jungho Yoo has obtained complementary production and cost data from the Korean automobile industry. Thus, our research work in Korea, the US and Japan has given us sufficient quantitative data to specify a reasonably accurate model of current production technologies for compact automobiles. This Appendix provides a description of the numbers and the modeling approach.

THE DATA BASE

For a case as complex as automobile production, it is necessary to make relatively precise assumptions about the degree of integration of the process being modeled. In the OECD countries, some plants simply assemble components which have been brought in from supplier units. At the opposite extreme are huge, integrated complexes which combine a whole range of activities – casting, forging, stamping, welding, engine and transmission production, painting, and final assembly. Since we are interested in estimating full unit costs for automobile production, we have chosen to use technology vectors representing operations which are highly integrated.

Fortunately, the information base which we have assembled seems sufficient to support such an exercise. During our research visit to

Japan, we received extraordinarily good cooperation from two major Japanese automobile producers – Toyota and Nissan. As a result, we obtained data on technologies for actual auto production operations in Japan. For Toyota, our numbers capture the main features of the Takaoka plant, which has been in operation (with considerable interim modernization) since 1966. This plant produces several Toyota models: Corolla, Sprinter, Corsa, Corolla II and Tercel. It has a capacity of 240 000 units/year and has shops engaged in stamping, welding, painting, and final assembly. In addition, we were provided with information on engine and transmission facilities which serve as feeders to the Takaoka plant.

In the case of Nissan, our numbers capture the main features of the Zama plant, which produces a variety of small vehicles. The Zama plant has a yearly capacity of about 430 000 units. Again, we were provided with data on standard assembly shop activities – stamping, welding, painting, and final assembly – as well as information on ancillary facilities for machining, transmissions, engines, etc.

At both Toyota and Nissan, we met with top production engineers who came fully prepared to answer detailed questions on staffing and costs. For understandable reasons, neither company was anxious to provide us with a complete picture of production economics within their plants. Both, however, were quite forthcoming about at least some of the required data. By combining the results of our Toyota and Nissan interviews, we were able to piece together a composite picture of a "typical" Japanese production facility.[24] We have labeled this "Semi-Automated" in our set of technology vectors, since Japanese plants are considerably more highly automated than their Korean counterpart operated by Hyundai. Both the Toyota Takaoka facility and the new Toyota/GM facility (NUMMI) in California produce Toyota Corolla models, and they seem to operate at about the same scale. We have therefore employed this scale in establishing our "Semi-Automated" auto technology vector. It should probably be thought of as representing typical practice in Japan, and current best practice in the US.

For Korea, we have obtained detailed standard input vectors for automobile production through the interviews of Dr Jungho Yoo. These vectors seem clearly to come from Hyundai's plant, and this is fortunate because it provides us with a good basis for comparing present and past Korean production conditions with those in Japan. From Hervey (1982), we have obtained standard production data from Hyundai in 1979 and 1981, and we have been greatly interested by the comparison with the numbers obtained by Dr. Yoo. The labor input data show that Hyundai is coming down the learning curve at a steady clip. From very high levels in the late 1970s, they have now descended to levels similar to those of a typical Japanese plant in 1979. Since then, of course, the Japanese themselves have made steady progress, albeit at a diminishing rate as they approach the learning frontier with their current technology.

Finally, we have specified a Robotic technology derived from extensive consultation with US and Japanese industry experts and published sources. Our Robotic technology represents the estimated capabilities and cost of state-of-the-art facilities at the end of the 1980s. Although we have prominently featured GM's Saturn complex in our discussion of emerging technologies, we do not think that it provides a completely satisfactory basis for specifying Robotic technology. GM has chosen an explicitly tutorial role for Saturn. Along with NUMMI, Saginaw, and other current projects, it will provide the launching point for corporate learning about robotic installations in the 1990s. We cannot, therefore, take the current public estimate of the plant's cost – $6 billion – seriously as an estimate for a "typical" robotic installation in the early 1990s. The current cost of the equipment in a typical Semi-Automated plant is in the neighborhood of $300 million. Given the consensus of industry experts about potential labor-saving in Robotic plants, it is not hard to deduce that a $6 billion Robotic compact car plant would not be cost-competitive with current Japanese operations.

We therefore believe that GM is embarking on its Saturn venture with the intention of amortizing its investment over a large number of other facilities. Our interview information leads us to believe that an investment in the range $1–2 billion (enormous in any case) is more appropriate for a typical first generation Robotic plant.

TECHNOLOGY VECTORS

Our basic input estimates for the three plant types are presented in Table A.4.1. As in the case of semiconductors and garments, our modeling approach does not force the model plants to begin at full capacity. Rather, they begin at relatively modest load factors and then move toward full capacity at variable rates, depending upon the underlying assumptions made about relative learning speeds. In this case, our assumptions about load factors are dictated by the data

TABLE A.4.1.   *Compact automobile assembly: three standard technologies*

	Manual	Semi-Automated	Robotic	
Capacity per day	800	960	2000	
Initial load factor	75	90	60	
Standard learning time (yrs.)	8	7	6	
Final load factor	95	96	97	
Operators	2800	2300	1500	
Technicians	220	100	250	
Engineers	110	80	200	
Overhead workers	2450	1500	1000	
Materials ($)	1800	1800	1800	
Equipment ($ million)	150	300	1000	(2000)
Land (acres)	400	400	400	
Plant size (sq. ft.)	440000	400000	300000	

sources. Our "Manual" technology is our representation of Hyundai's facility, and we therefore posit a relatively low initial load factor to reflect the fact that Hyundai is still relatively high on the learning curve. Our "Semi-Automated" technology, on the other hand, represents current mature production conditions in Japan (or transplanted by Japanese management to the US). It therefore has a high initial load factor. Finally, we posit a substantially lower initial load factor for the Robotic technology, since companies installing it will just be starting down a new learning curve.

Our learning time and load factor estimates reflect what is currently known about the dynamic behavior of production in each technology class. Our treatment of the Robotic numbers reflects, for example, the fact that much of the skill content of production will be embodied in the machinery. Thus, the system should evolve toward a high load factor relatively rapidly. We posit a very large production capacity for the Robotic plant. Our manual technology behaves in the opposite way: it evolves toward maximum load at a slower rate, and the attainable maximum itself is lower.

The labor input numbers for the three technologies reflect the operation of two sets of forces. The first is standard capital-labor substitution in the face of sharply differing relative input prices. From the Hyundai numbers to the Toyota/Nissan motors, there is a sharp fall-off in direct labor and overhead workers, coupled with an approximate doubling of equipment expenditure. This is as it should be in theory; it reflects the operation of all the productivity-related factors as discussed earlier.

The concurrent decline in engineers and technicians seems like an anomaly, however. We would normally expect to see intellectual capital, embodied in technical staff, to increase with physical capital. In fact, the numbers become quite sensible when the role of learning is properly understood. At present, Japanese auto technology is much more mature than that of Korea. In our interviews at Toyota, the engineering personnel noted that Toyota has a sizable central engineering staff whose personnel are assigned to new production operations during their startup period. Once the new system is in place, the central engineering staff members withdraw and a relatively modest number of plant-specific engineers and technicians is retained. Under current conditions at Hyundai, of course, quite a different situation prevails. Hyundai is making vigorous efforts to move down the learning curve, and it makes perfect sense for there to be a sizable engineering-technical staff on hand.

In the Korean and Japanese engineer/technician numbers, we therefore see the combination of two forces: Relative investment in learning about the installed technology, and routine activities associated with the operation of that technology. At the same point on the learning curve, we might still expect to see more Korean engineers and technicians (they are, after all, much lower paid than their Japanese counterparts), but the numbers would undoubtedly be closer.

For the Robotic technology, we have registered the substantial increase in engineers and technicians which all industry experts note will be associated with the routine operation of a highly-automated plant. If anything, our engineer/technician numbers are probably conservative. Here it is also worthwhile noting the huge jump in capital cost (from $300 million to $1 billion) associated with movement to Robotic technology. As we noted previously, this estimate is actually quite conservative. At the present state of implementation of computer-integrated manufacturing (which is sparse), $2 billion many be more realistic. We have therefore run simulations for this higher investment level, as well.

INPUT COSTS

Our model requires many numbers pertaining to country-specific input costs and future growth rates. Table A.4.2 includes the relevant estimates for the automobile industries of Korea, the US and Japan. Our Korean numbers are derived from Dr Yoo's interviews, and the US and Japanese numbers have been gleaned from our own interviews and from standard industry sources.

Certain input numbers are striking, particularly the relatively long hours and low wages of the Korean workers. These are also reflected in Korea's low building costs. Some compensation is provided by Korea's relatively high interest rate and by markup to reflect the fact that a substantial portion of auto production equipment and inputs are still imported. Finally, it is worth noting Japan's high land price, which reflects the scarcity of space in the Tokyo-Osaka corridor. Japanese auto companies could move to other areas in the islands, of course, but they have shown little inclination to do so thus far. Our estimated growth rates for input prices are simply guesses, but seem to reflect the current consensus at each potential production site.

TABLE A.4.2. *Country-specific input data: automobile cost model. All prices in $US at the specified exchange rate.*

	Korea	US	Japan
Daily wage for operators ($)	29	180	200
Daily wage for technicians ($)	47	200	231
Daily wage for engineers ($)	40	220	278
Daily wage for overhead workers ($)	34	160	215
Working days per year	300	250	250
Working hours per day	10	8	8
Building construction price ($/sq.ft.)	33	100	154
Interest rate (%)	10	8	6
Years for depreciating equipment	10	10	10
Years for depreciating structures	40	40	40
Exchange rate ($U.S.)	800	1	120
Land price ($'000/acre)	130	150	300
Anticipated growth rate of prices and wages (%)	5	4	4
Markup for imported equipment and inputs (%)	10	0	0

5 Conclusions

Two recent developments have significantly broadened the domain of international competition. The diffusion of microelectronics is rapidly increasing the range of technological choice. At the same time, several major new aspirants, particularly the largest Asian nations, are bidding for larger shares of international markets. In this book we have used three sectoral case-studies to analyze the potential competitive impact of these new forces.

The case studies evoke several common themes. The availability of microelectronics technologies has potentially improved the competitiveness of the advanced industrial countries. Particularly in cases where these countries have a significant lead in the adopting of such technologies, they will be able to produce at lower costs and higher quality levels for markets with high income elasticities.

Microelectronics reduces the need for direct labor, and this is an obvious advantage. However, in some cases the advantage stems from a more fundamental source: the absolute superiority of the technology. Even though the new technologies are more capital intensive, they use less capital *and* labor per unit of output. They also create increased possibilities for product differentiation, a factor which we have not explored extensively in this book.

In many cases, of course, the new technologies have not enhanced measured productivity as rapidly as had originally been hoped. Part of the difficulty may be purely metric: Conventional accounting methods ignore the increased process flexibility and product quality which can accompany the introduction of microelectronics based systems. These methods almost certainly understate the true value of microelectronics' ultimate contribution to profitability.

However, microelectronics is not always efficiency-enhancing, nor is it always easy to incorporate into the production system. Some firms have wasted large amounts by giving too little thought to the choice of appropriate systems and the timing of their introduction. Consider, for example the history of recent industrial experiments at General Motors. As we noted in Chapter 4, GM rushed into microelectronics based systems in an attempt to leapfrog its competitors. In the face of repeated delays, cost overruns, and systems difficulties, GM now admits that it should have proceeded at a less exuberant pace.[1] It has undoubtedly been chastened as well by its concurrent experience with NUMMI, the General Motors-Toyota joint venture in California. Superior management has made NUMMI the most productive unit in the GM system despite its relative technological "backwardness".

The NUMMI experience points to another major source of competitive advantage. Much of the superior performance of the Japanese system can be attributed to its flexibility. NUMMI has made it clear that flexibility gave Japanese firms competitive advantage long before the advent of sophisticate microelectronic systems, although it is clear that such systems can enhance flexibility.

Despite these cautionary notes, we do find that the new technologies may profoundly affect existing patterns of trade. Their productive potential will shore up the competitive positions of Western firms in many markets, not all of them highly income-elastic. Some surprising developments may soon occur in sectors whose maturity and traditional labor intensity have consigned them to "sunset" status in the minds of many Western economists. The major example from our case studies is that of garments. In garments, automation will soon progress to the point where US firms, under existing tariff legislation, will have the potential for a return to profitable production in many product lines which have been lost to East Asian competitors. For apparel products or production stages which remain resistant to full automation, US producers will have the option of establishing process links with Caribbean, Mexican or Central American sites where rapid market response times are preserved.

Similarly, under the influence of rapid progress in microelectronics, automobile production has the potential for rejoining semiconductors as an "immature" industrial process. Computer assisted design (CAD) and computer integrated manufacturing (CIM), along with newly integrated communications and information links between sellers and suppliers, have allowed technologically progressive manufacturers in the OECD markets to launch themselves down new organizational learning curves. As a result, our model results suggest that robotic production of compact automobiles in North America will be cost-competitive with current Korean offerings by the mid-1990s. In fact, the results show that Japanese production using semi-automated technology is already so efficient that Korean producers will be at a slight cost disadvantage until they come somewhat further down the learning curve.

The challenge for the newly industrializing countries (NICs) lies in adapting to this rapid pace of change. The period of exploiting cheap labor is now over and technological sophistication is going to be increasingly important. Some NICs, particularly Korea and Taiwan, have already launched major drives to acquire technological capability in the area of semiconductors, systems engineering, advanced machine tools, robotics and telecommunications.

Much of the initiative in Korea is coming from the large Korean conglomerates, which have already achieved some success in products which are technically not very demanding (microcomputers, for example). The government has been particularly active in developing new communications infrastructure: Korea is rapidly acquiring sophisticated capabilities in both voice and data communications. This capability will give it a competitive advantage in many manufacturing and service industries.

Similar initiatives on Taiwan have been somewhat hampered by differences in organizational scale: Taiwanese firms are generally smaller than their Korean counterparts. However, the larger Taiwanese firms are acquiring a systems engineering capability for implementing the new technologies. The Taiwanese government is supplementing these efforts by promoting the communications sector and funding broad-based research and development.

Another theme which emerges repeatedly in our case studies is the importance of strategic behavior by firms and governments. Rapid shifts in currency regimes, quota arrangements (implicit or explicit), and protectionist sentiment can have short-run effects which dominate the influence of other factors. The impact of the recent yen shock on the competitiveness of North American automobile production has been documented in Chapter 4.

The semiconductor industry has also been affected. Our analysis of the advanced memory market in Chapter 3 concluded that under the traditional competitive rules, Korea's attempt to become a major player was financially ill-considered at this time. As in the case of automobiles and garments, however, the politics of protection and international finance have had a profound influence on Korean prospects. With drastic appreciation of the Yen and Korea's refusal to countenance a major revaluation of the Won, Korean memory producers have received a shot in the arm. Probably more important, however, has been the US-Japan semiconductor pact. This agreement, in deliberate restraint of trade and production, has prompted large price increases for memory chips. Our calculations suggest that

Korean firms can now at least break even with the current generation of advanced chips, even if they are substantially higher on the learning curve than their US and Japanese counterparts. With the advent of a new generation of chips, however, their difficulties may well re-emerge.

Korea's current commitment to high-level competition in all three sectors considered in this book suggests the ambition to become a full player in international industrial society more rapidly than any previous aspirant. Undeniably, the results of Korea's initiatives to date have been impressive. Korea has been strong as a textile and garment producer; it has enjoyed preliminary success in the export of a first-generation compact automobile to the North American market; and it has become one of the few economies with strong competence in the fabrication of basic semiconductor memories. An uncritical look at the current level of activity would certainly suggest a rosy outlook. Unfortunately, this outlook is not supported by an examination of current trends in technology, world labor supply, and strategic behavior by governments and dominant firms in the OECD countries.

The challenge to Korea and the other NICs comes from all sides: advanced industrial nations, new aspirants to middle-income NIC status (Thailand and Malaysia, for example), and the low-wage countries. The new aspirants have lower labor costs than Korea and Taiwan but already see the need to move upscale technologically. How successful they will be in this attempt at technological leapfrogging is difficult to assess at present. Much will depend on the provision of the type of infrastructure that Korea and Taiwan are trying to develop.

While cheaper information capital moves comparative advantage in the direction of OECD producers in certain product lines, cheaper basic labor moves it toward the Asian population giants in others. At remarkably proximate points in time, all of the present and future population giants of Asia – China, India, Bangladesh, Pakistan, and Indonesia – have become much more interested in world market competition. All have an abundance of labor which is far cheaper than in the NICs or in the countries we have labelled "new aspirants"; and the two largest, China and India, have ample reservoirs of well-trained, low-wage engineering and technical workers as well.

In some subsectors of textile/garment production, it is currently apparent that only a worldwide system of quotas and restrictions prevents Chinese producers from eliminating all competitors, including those in the US and East Asia. Here, the NICs suffer from a double disadvantage. In sectors where labor-intensive modes at Chinese labor costs dominate all currently-forseeable automated technologies, US producers will undoubtedly be shored up by entry restrictions. The fortunes of Korean and Taiwanese producers, on the other hand, will be subject to the whims of the US political system. If entry quotas for textiles are generalized, for example, they will have a difficult time withstanding competition from China and other low wage producers.

The problem of strategic interaction is in fact much broader than simple protectionism in the US garment sector. The Japanese seem entirely serious about protecting their hard-won competitive advantage in semiconductor memories and automobiles. Concentration is growing in the US garment and textile industries; semiconductor memories and compact automobiles are produced by a relative handful of large, politically-powerful firms. They have all been badly bruised by East Asian market entrants in the past decade, and they are now inclined to take entry-level competition much more seriously than in the past.

Their political leverage, combined with the favorable impact of microelectronics on cost-competitiveness and the presence of the Japanese as powerful players, suggests that the NICs' major hope lies in rapid growth of the US market. If market size is relatively fixed (or even receding, as is possible in compact automobiles), the struggle by the dominant firms to retain share will undoubtedly spell a sustained period of nearly-profitless production for firms located in the NICs. Under such circumstances, a policy of promoting strategic alliances with incumbent US or Japanese firms might serve their interests better than direct competition.

In the United States, there is currently much discussion of the prospect of a "shrinking middle" in the income distribution, as the advent of cheap information capital reduces the demand for painstakingly-developed industrial skills. Our analysis suggests that similar trends are emerging internationally, and that the NICs may now find the period of their meteoric rise into the international middle class succeeded by an era in which growth expectations become more modest.

Which is not to say, of course, that any economic catastrophe looms on the horizon. The NICs have developed their industrial and technical resources so rapidly in recent years that their success has become a model for many developing societies. They will undoubtedly continue to build a solid future as major industrial states with steadily deepening human resources and industrial/technical capabilities.

As is frequently the case in human affairs, however, much remains in the lap of fortune. The simultaneous and massive entry of cheap robots and cheap workers into world markets during the next decade will subject the NICs to unprecedented challenges. Among our sectors, the short-run betting odds for the NICs seem relatively unfavorable in advanced semiconductor memories and garments. They are somewhat better in textiles, and reasonably favorable in compact automobiles. Much will turn, however, on the growth of markets in the West, the persistence of entrepreneurial energy there, and the vigor with which the Japanese decide to defend the outposts of their industrial empire.

Notes

1 Competitive Advantage in the Information Age

1. In our view, insight into the changing patterns of international location and trade requires a greater degree of disaggregation than has generally been adopted. Conventional measures of productivity change may grossly understate the impact of new technologies. See Bresnahan (1986); Flamm (1987); Trajtenberg (1985).
2. We have discussed product cycles mainly in terms of exogenous technical change. However, in some markets, the dominant firms may be able to control the product cycle by setting industry standards and changing these standards in response to internal profit considerations.
3. See Jaffe (1986) for an empirical application of the idea of technological neighborhoods.
4. See Wilson (1981).
5. Including implicit payments to trading enterprises which often serve as market intermediaries. See Levy (1987) for recent evidence on Taiwan and Korea.
6. Recent analyses have argued that the Korean and Taiwanese paths may both represent economically rational responses to differing initial conditions. See Mody (1986); Levy/Kuo (1987a,b).
7. According to the World Bank's standard projection (see the *World Development Report*, 1984, Table 1), these five countries will have 47 per cent of the total population of countries outside the OECD and Comecon blocs in the year 2050. Africa will account for a substantial proportion of the remainder. Many African states have also become more outwardly-oriented in recent years.
8. Institutional development may be thought of as the overcoming of market failures in order to adequately mobilize available resources. Such mobilization is necessary but not sufficient to effectively compete in international markets.
9. See Kamien and Schwartz (1972).
10. See Evans (1985a,b).
11. The new pattern unfolding in the aftermath of the Yen shock is not clear as yet. Japanese firms will not be able to automate fast enough to preserve competitive advantage in all product lines at Japanese production sites. Part of the response has been to shift investments more rapidly toward market-orientated production sites in the US and Western Europe. Another part has been an upsurge of purchase and subcontract arrangements with firms in Korea, Taiwan, and elsewhere. A new 'trailing edge' has emerged from Japanese industry, and its outline is now becoming discernible.
12. Brander and Spencer (1985).
13. For a more complete analysis, see Chapter 3 and Mody/Wheeler (1987b).

2 The Garment and Textile Industries

1. This chapter draws on Mody and Wheeler (1987a).
2. When these categories are further disaggregated, it is seen that in some of the sub-categories the import/production ratio has fallen somewhat.
3. It should be noted that the *absolute values* of Philippine exports do not reflect the world pattern; while Europe is the largest source of garment import demand, Philippine exports are very largely concentrated in the US market.
4. See Rhee *et al* (1984): "In some Korean industries without obvious technical economies of scale, firms are very large. This can probably be best explained by the advantages of such firms in dealing with large foreign buyers."
5. The VER is supposed to "spring spontaneously from the exporter" and the OMA "is based on bilateral negotiations". This difference in legality does not have much economic significance. See Jones (1983).
6. Comprehensive histories of the various arrangements can be found in General Agreement on Tariffs and Trade (1984) and Keesing/Wolf (1980). There is a continuing literature in the pages of the *Journal of World Trade Law* and the *World Economy*. The costs of such protection to developed country consumers have been studied by, among others, Pelzman (1982); Cline (1987).
7. In a recent study UNCTAD has estimated that reduction of tariff barriers in the EEC, US and Japan would increase apparel exports to these countries by 50 per cent and the elimination of non-tariff distortions would increase exports by a further 60 per cent. See UNCTAD (1986).
8. See GATT, op. cit., Tables 3.13 and 3.14, pp. 93–98.
9. See Rottenberg (1985).
10. According to available evidence, there has been a growing trend towards smaller and more frequent orders from retailers.
11. There has been some success in achieving flexibility within narrowly defined product categories and much less success in achieving flexibility across these categories. As discussed in the text, this has led to specialization in sub-sectors of the apparel and textile industry.
12. On recent merger activity in Britain, see *Financial Times*, 12 February 1986.
13. That is, a process combining Pre-Assembly in the US, Assembly in China, and Post-Assembly in the US would involve substantially more transit time than a process which linked US Pre- and Post-Assembly to Assembly in the Caribbean.
14. Under the 807 regulations, only value added outside the US is taxed. The tariff burden can therefore be quite light for garments produced from US textiles, pre-assembled in the US, assembled in the Caribbean, and post-assembled back in the US. Since the tariff rates on some garments are more than 40 per cent, the difference in final product cost can be very substantial.
15. It is of interest, for example, to contrast these with current estimates of the capital cost of a move from Semi-Automated ($300 million) to Robotic ($1–2 billion) production in compact automobiles. Flexible

automation for automobile assembly is a much harder engineering problem.

16. The term "load factor" refers to the proportion of theoretical capacity which is actually achieved by a plant.

17. The major integrated garment manufactuers have structured their operations to take these economies into account. Arrow Shirts, one of the largest US producers, maintains one Pre-Assembly plant in Atlanta, Georgia which feeds pieces to a large number of Assembly operations in the region. There are numerous other examples which highlight this substantial asymmetry in economies of scale between Pre-Assembly and later phases of garment production.

18. Although we combine robotic sewing and UPS in our model of automated technology, UPS systems can be operated in conjunction with less advanced garment assembly technologies.

19. Since our product-specific data are extremely detailed, the model can make realistic calculations of transport costs. The appropriate unit for air and sea transport cost in the garment case is volume, and we have appropriate volume measures for our six garment products. They differ considerably because of differences in garment bulk and packing arrangements. We also have established air and sea transport cost schedules for our routing pairs.

20. The computer results displayed in Table 2.5 have been generated using the assumption that fabric is available everywhere (including Korea) at the cost of production in China, the current least-cost producer. Since fabrics are traded internationally, this is not an unreasonable assumption. Our interest here is in analyzing competitive status in garment production alone.

21. Here Jamaica is used to represent several Caribbean states which are increasing in importance as garment production sites. Mexican and Central American locations have similar characteristics.

22. In this chapter our use of the term "Caribbean" implies inclusion of Mexico and the Central American countries.

23. Our modeling results also suggest that they have now had an economic incentive to do what the US has traditionally done: form joint production arrangements with low-wage sewing operations in the Caribbean.

3 The NIC Challenge in Advanced Electronics

1. This chapter draws on Mody (1986; 1987) and Mody and Wheeler (1986; 1987b).

2. Though we have stressed the similarities between Korea and Taiwan, there are important differences which are discussed in Mody (1986).

3. *Business Week*, 24 September 1986, pp. 88–91. Daewoo's Model D PC received a "Best Buy" rating from Consumer Reports. The competitive strength of Korean PCs has been described widely in the commercial press; see, for example, *Business Digest of Southern New Jersey*, May 1986, pp. 18, 21 and *The Wall Street Journal*, 6 November 1986, p. 12.

4. *News Release*, 29 July 1986, p. 1.

5. See *Korea Herald*, 14 December 1983; 21 February 1984.

6. None of the developed countries has an explicit market reserve policy; however, a procurement preference in effect provides a market reserve. Commenting on US electronics policy, Nelson (1984, p. 68) has argued that US producers had a large protected domestic market because of government procurement policies.

7. For the first seven months of 1986, Samsung made only $25 million of profits on electronics-related sales of $1.23 billion. The low profits are partial evidence of cross-subsidy. The possiblity of dumping charges comes not merely from the US but also from the European Community (see *Electronics Engineering Times*, 20 October 1986, p. 10).

8. There is a large literature on the Brazilian computer industry: Tigre (1983), Evans (1985a,b), Adler (1986), and Ramamurthi (1985). Our description here is based primarily on the papers by Evans.

9. One indication of restriction of technology flow from Japan to Korea is the prevalence in Seoul of weekend "moonlighting" by Japanese engineers.

10. 'Foreign telecommunications companies are welcome, but they have learned that they must work with a local partner and they must meet some very demanding technology transfer conditions' *(Business Korea,* May 1986, p. 18).

11. *Business Korea,* May 1986, pp. 18–29.

12. The "K" and "M" stand respectively for Kilobytes (1000 bits) and Megabytes (1 million bits). The bit is the unit of storage and is either a 0 or a 1. Thus a 256K DRAM will store 256 000 1's and 0's.

13. We shall not describe these manufacturing stages in detail, but several good explanations are readily available. See, for example, Fischetti (1984); Gise and Blanchard (1979); Sze (1983); and Bowlby (1985).

14. The estimated costs do not include overheads.

15. The cabinet-level Trade Policy group was created in September 1985 by President Reagan in response to complaints of unfair trade practices against US producers. The 256K complaint represented the first action of the group.

16. Since we have controlled for pretty nearly everything, the superiority of the Japanese performance reflects principally the earlier start.

17. Persistent loud complaints in the US industry about inability to "make any money" in 256K DRAM production seem to have reflected reality, if our numbers are roughly correct.

18. The discussion in this subsection is based mainly on the *Electronic Engineering Times* Report (20 January 1986), written by Girish Mhatre.

19. *EE Times*, op. cit., p.34.

20. Tom Balch of TI in *EE Times*.

21. *EE Times*, op. cit., p.34.

22. *EE Times*, op. cit., p. 34.

23. The Japanese companies are: Hitachi, Oki, Fujitsu, Toshiba, Matsushita, NEC, Mitsubishi and Sharp of Japan and Samsung of Korea.

24. *Electronics*, 3 February 1986, p. 20. "TI claims to have 150 US patents applicable to DRAM production. It cited eight registered US patents, dating from 1970 to 1985, in the suit against the Korean and Japanese

companies. The patents cover a binary decoder; a high-density, high-speed, random-access read-write memory; high-speed sense amplifiers for MOS RAMs; a RAM cell with different capacitor and transistor oxide thicknesses; an integrated-circuit MOS capacitor using implanted regions to change thresholds; carrier packaging for ICs; and two high-performance dynamic sense amplifiers with voltage boost for row-address lines". (*Electronics*, 3 February 1986, pp. 19–20).

25. *Electronics*, 3 February 1986, pp. 19–20.
26. In the computer and peripherals industry, Tandon has recently won out of court settlements whereby Sony and Teac will pay royalties for the use of technology that Tandon claims to have patented. IBM has been seeking to control the growth of its Japanese counterparts by stressing its intellectual primacy.
27. *Electronics*, 27 January 1986, p. 60. The computer industry has probably the largest proliferation of strategic partnerships. These include links between Amdahl and Fujitsu, Hitachi and National Semiconductor, AT&T, Olivetti, Goldstar and Toshiba, Honeywell, Groupe Bull and NEC. For details see *Computerworld*, 9 December 1985, p. 66.
28. *Electronic Engineering Times*, 17 February 1986, p. 1.
29. Another recent partnership has been formed between two US firms: National Semiconductor and Xerox. The two are expected to exchange technology for the development of CMOS application specific integrated circuits (*Electronic Engineering Times*, 17 February 1986, p. 1.)
30. Founder and President of DM Data, Inc., Scottsdale, Arizona.
31. Note that there is no real difference between this time-dependent model and the classic experience curve model under the assumption of steady production. The latter posits a relation between cumulative volume and cost declines, which is no more than a time-dependent specification under the assumption of constant activity.

4 The Automobile Industry

1. According to one recent estimate (Taylor, 1987), 175 automakers produced over 45 million cars, trucks, and buses last year. Total sales were approximately $384 billion – 2.1 per cent of world GNP.
2. *Far East Economic Review*, 3 October 1985.
3. To cite a recent study (Salter *et al.*, 1985): "Even under the most benign industry conditions, auto competition is a game of high costs and engineering complexity, complicated by cyclical industry sales. It is an industry dominated by economies of scale, where decisions to increase or decrease production must be made in increments of thousands of units and millions of dollars ... A single new car line can cost as much as $4 billion and take five years to move from concept to production ... In addition, a single project can require the participation of as many as 30 000 suppliers."
4. *Financial Times*, 21 July 1987.
5. *Far East Economic Review*, 3 October 1985, p. 73.

6. See Womack (1986).
7. See Gooding (1987); Fisher (1987).
8. Korean effort and sacrifice levels continue to impress foreign observers. One industry analyst whom we interviewed was particular struck by the fact that a Korean assembly plant which he had visited in 1985 was unheated. This sort of thing, coupled with double 10-hour shifts per day and 6-day work weeks, is what makes OECD producers nervous. The recent round of strikes and labor negotiations has reduced Korea's competitive advantage somewhat, as will be shown later in the chapter.
9. In this context, it is of interest to note that favorable reviews of the Hyundai Excel have contained no complaints about "fit and finish". The apparently acceptable polish of the Excel contrasts with the following observation from an industry consultant who toured Korean auto plants in 1982: "We saw any number of examples of bad fits among the various body components being brought into the body assembly operation. The use of hammers to bring body components together was quite prevalent and is usually a bad sign. There apparently is a significant amount of tolerance buildup in either the original design of parts and/or the stamping, tooling or due to wear on the various tooling elements. These must be eliminated if a quality vehicle is to be built" (Hervey, 1982).
10. Interview with Leroy Lindgren, February 1986.
11. See Inggrassia (1987).
12. *Business Week*, 3 March 1986, p. 39.
13. Yuge (1987).
14. There is little doubt that the Koreans intend to follow the Japanese. Korean auto company spokesmen are already beginning to discuss plans for the introduction of upscale models in the US market. See Beauchamp (1986).
15. At the current value of the Yen (Y. 120–130/$US) our cost model suggests that Japanese production of compact units in Japan has lost its competitive advantage. Japanese production in the US is currently lowest-cost.
16. It remains to be seen, of course, whether the Japanese-Korean productivity differential in this stylized example is representative of the true differential in compact auto production. Our quantitative analysis of this question, draws on our dynamic unit cost model.
17. Current evidence suggests that the Japanese production system also operates successfully under North American conditions. One industry analyst whom we interviewed voiced the opinion that Honda's auto plant in Marysville, Ohio is currently the most efficient facility in the world. Current operations by Nissan (Smyrna, Tennessee) and Toyota/GM (NUMMI–Fremont, California) are also meeting with a success which has considerably surpassed initial expectations.
18. GM, with a world market share of 18.1 percent in 1986, is by far the largest of the group. Ford is next, with a 13.3 percent share. Chrysler, by contrast, had a share of 4.9 percent (Taylor, 1987).
19. According to *Business Week*, 3 March 1986, "The Big Three ... appear to have given up trying to produce their cheapest models in the US.

General Motors Corp. buys its lowest-priced cars from Suzuki Motors Co., and the company admits its vaunted Saturn will probably debut in 1990 as a relatively pricy small car, rather than the budget model originally planned. Ford Motor Co. is thinking of turning production of replacements for its best-selling small cars, the Escort and Lynx, over to its Japanese partner, Mazda Motor Corp., by 1990. Even Chrysler Corp., which is ballyhooing a $5,400 'America' version of its aging Omni and Horizon subcompacts, admits the cars will be canceled next year so that it can tool up for more expensive replacements.

20. Howard Kehrl, GM's vice chairman, recalls that GM's executives in mid-1981 were near a decision to build a new "S-body" car, to be introduced in 1984. During the deliberations, a GM cost study concluded that the Japanese could build the same car for $2,000 less, largely because Japanese production methods were far more efficient. "We said, 'This is crazy,' and that's how Saturn was born," relates Kehrl. (*US News and World Report*, 5 August 1985, p. 23).

21. In a recent interview, GM's President was queried about looking more to overseas sources for components. His response: "No. That's not our game plan ... As a matter of fact, I can think of some parts we're bringing back in from Singapore – radio production – into Kokomo (Indiana) because we've automated. Working with the people and the processes in the plant we've been able to beat the Singapore labor rates. That's what we'd like to do."

22. These data take account of the Japanese "Yen shock" and the recent Korean "wage shock."

23. For arranging extremely valuable interviews with senior Japanese industry engineers and executives, we are particularly indebted to the following people: Dr Saburo Okita, formerly Foreign Minister of Japan; Dr. Keichi Oshima, Professor Emeritus, University of Tokyo; Professor Shigeru Ishikawa, Aoyama Gakuin University.

24. We have also subjected our labor input numbers to a simple plausibility test: we have calculated typical input hours by activity (e.g. stamping, welding, painting, final assembly) in 1978 for our model Japanese plant by "back-casting" our labor input numbers to 1978 under the assumption of normal (4–5%) labor productivity growth. We have compared our "backcasts" with results published by the Japanese Ministry of Labor (1978), and are satisfied that our current depiction of manning in a typical Japanese plant is reasonable.

5 Conclusions

1. Dorothy Leonard-Barton (1987a,b), among others, has extensively documented the difficulties of incorporating microelectronics technologies into production and design systems.

Bibliography

Abernathy, W.C.J., *et al* (1981) "The New Industrial Competition", *Harvard Business Review*, 59(5), pp. 68–81.

Adler, Immanuel (1986) "Brazil's Domestic Computer Strategy", *International Organization*, 40(3), pp. 673–707.

Allen, Bruce (1985) *Microelectronics, Employment, and Labor in the North American Automobile Industry*, Working Paper, ILO World Employment Programme Research (ILO: Geneva).

American Apparel Manufacturers Association (1985) *Focus: economic profile of the apparel industry*, AAMA, Arlington, VA.

American Apparel Manufacturers Association (1985) *Apparel manufacturing strategies*, AAMA, Arlington, VA.

Baily, Martin, and Alok Chakrabarti (1985) "Productivity Growth Slowdown by US Industry", *Brookings Papers on Economic Activity*, 2, pp. 423–59.

Beauchamp, Marc (1986) "Foot in the Door", *Forbes*, December 29.

Boston Consulting Group (1985) *Comparison of retail-related costs: domestic versus Far East*, Boston, February.

Bowlby, Reed (1985) "The DIP May Take its Final Bows", IEEE Spectrum, pp. 37–42, June.

Brander, James, and Barbara Spencer (1985) "Export Subsidies and International Market Share Rivalry", *Journal of International Economics*, pp. 83–100.

Bresnahan, Timothy (1986) "Measuring the Spillovers from Technical Advance: Mainframe Computers in Financial Services", *American Economic Review*, 76, September, pp. 742–55.

Clarke, Bryan (1984) "Robotics in the Sewing Room", *Bobbin*, November, pp. 208–12.

Cline, William (1987) *The Future of World Trade in Textiles and Apparel*, Institute for International Economics, Washington.

Cole, Robert (ed.) (1983) *Automobiles and the Future: Competition, Cooperation, and Change*, Ann Arbor: Michigan Papers in Japanese Studies, No. 10.

Cole, Robert, and Yakushiji, T. (1984) *The American and Japanese Auto Industries in Transition*, Ann Arbor: Center for Japanese Studies.

Cotton, Richard (1986) *U.S. Apparel Competitiveness: Today's Opportunity*, mimeo., February 18.

Downs, Thomas W. (1986) "Using the User Cost", *Journal of Economics and Business*, 38, No. 4, pp. 297–305.

Evans, Peter (1985a) "Varieties of Nationalism: the Politics of the Brazilian Computer Industry", in Antonio Botelho and Peter Smith (eds.) *The Computer Question in Brazil: High Technology in a Developing Society*, Center for International Studies, MIT.

Evans, Peter (1985b) "State, Capital, and the Transformation of Dependence: the Brazilian Computer Case", Center for Comparative Study of Development, Brown University.

Evenson, Robert (1984) "International Invention: Implications for Technology Market Analysis", in Griliches (1984).

Finan, W. and Lamond, A (1985) "Sustaining U.S. Competitiveness in Microelectronics: The Challenge to U.S. Policy", in B. Scott and G. Lodge (eds.) *Competitiveness in the World Economy*, Boston: Harvard Business School Press, Chap. 3, pp. 144–75.

Fischetti. M.A. (1984) "Technology '84: Solid State", IEEE Spectrum, January, pp. 58–63.

Fisher, Andrew (1987) "Life beyond a scandal: Andrew Fisher talks to Carl Hahn, chairman of Volkswagen", *Financial Times,* July 1.

Flamm, Kenneth (1987) *Targeting the Computer: Government Support and International Competition*, Washington: The Brookings Institution.

Flynn, Michael (1985) "U.S. and Japanese Automotive Productivity Comparisons: Strategic Implications", *National Productivity Review*, Winter, pp. 60–71.

Frazier, Robert M. (1985) "New Technology helps apparel manufacturers capitalize on the U.S. advantage with quick response", AAMA Bobbin Show, Atlanta, GA, September 10.

Friedlaender, Ann, *et al* (1983) "Costs, Technology, and Productivity in the U.S. Automobile Industry," *Bell Journal of Economics*, 14(1), pp. 1–21.

Frischtak, Claudio (1986) "Brazil", in Francis W. Rushing and Carole Ganz Brown (eds.), *National Policies for Developing High Technology Industries: International Comparisons*, Westview Press, Boulder and London.

Fujimoto, Takahiro (1983a) *Technology Systems: A Comparison of the U.S. and Japanese Automobile Industries*, Working Paper, Mitsubishi Research Institute, Tokyo.

Fujimoto, Takahiro (1983b) *Automotive Industries in the Third World: Their Dynamics and Prospects*, Working Paper, Mitsubishi Research Institute, Tokyo.

Gaetan, Manuel (1984) "Worldwide Technology Update", *Bobbin*, July, pp. 46–62.

General Agreement on Tariffs and Trade (1984) *"Textiles and clothing in the world economy"*, Geneva.

Geroski, P.A. and A. Jacquemin (1984) "Dominant Firms' Alleged Decline" *International Journal of Industrial Organization*, 2, pp. 1–27.

Ghemawat, Pankaj (1985) "Building Strategy on the Experience Curve", *Harvard Business Review*, March–April, pp. 143–49.

Gise, P., and R. Blanchard (1979) "Semiconductor and Integrated Circuit Fabrication Techniques", Reston Publishing Company Inc., Reston, Va.

Gooding, Kenneth (1987) "Ford profits from forging links with competitors", *Financial Times*, September 22.

Government of Australia, Department of Industry, Technology and Commerce (1985) *Technology Prospects and Some Implications for the Apparel Manufacturing Industry in Australia*, Canberra ACT 2600, November.

Griliches, Zvi (ed.) (1984) *R&D Patents and Productivity*, National Bureau of Economic Research and the University of Chicago Press.

Hall, R. and Jorgensen, D.W. (1967) "Tax Policy and Investment Behavior", *American Economic Review*, 57, pp. 391–414.

Harbour, J.E., *et al.* *(1981) Productivity and Comparative Cost Advantages: Some Estimates for Major Automotive Producers*, Working Paper, Harvard Business School.

Hervey, Richard (1982) *Technology-Based Export Development and Import Substitution Strategies for the Korean Automotive Industry*, Consulting Study for the Korean Institute of Machinery and Metals by Sigma Associates, Management Consultants.

Hervey, Richard (1985) "GM's Strategies: Revolutionizing and Institutionalizing Change", *Paper presented at SITEV 85, Geneva, Switzerland, June 6.*

Hoffman, Kurt (1985) "Clothing Chips and Competitive Advantage: The Impact of Microelectronics on Trade and Production in the Garment Industry", *World Development*, 13, No. 3, pp. 371–92.

Hoffman, Kurt and Howard Rush (1988) *Microelectronics and Clothing, The Impact of Technical Change on a Global Industry*, New York: Praegers.

Inggrassia, Paul (1987) "U.S. Auto Makers get Chance to Regain Sales From Foreign Rivals", *Asian Wall Street Journal*, April 16, pp. 1,12.

Integrated Circuit Engineering Corporation (ICE), *Status 1985: A Report on the Integrated Circuit Industry*, (also *Status 1980–Status 1984*).

International Textile Manufacturers Federation (1983) *International Production Cost Comparison: Spinning/Weaving* (Geneva: ITMF).

International Textile Manufacturers Federation (1985) *International Production Cost Comparison: Spinning/Weaving* (Geneva: ITMF).

Jaffe, Adam B. (1986) "Technological Opportunity and Spillovers of R&D: Evidence from Firms' Patents, Profits, and Market Value", *American Economic Review*, 76, No. 3, pp. 984–1001.

Jones, Kent (1983) "The Political Economy of Voluntary Export Restraint Agreements", *Kyklos*, Vol. 37, pp. 82–101.

Kamien, Morton and Nancy Schwartz (1972) "Limit Pricing and Uncertain Entry", *Econometrica*, 39, pp. 441–454.

Keesing, D.B. and M. Wolf (1980) "Textile Quotas Against Developing Countries", Thames Essay No. 23, Trade Policy Research Centre, London.

Keller, Maryann (1986) "A Look at the Korean Auto Industry", in M.N. Keller (ed.) *Automotive Studies*, New York: Josephthal & Co.

Kim, P.S. (1985) "CMP Industry Analysis: Telecommunications", U.S. Embassy, Seoul.

Kurt Salmon Associates (1984) *Sourcing '84* (New York: KSA).

Kurt Salmon Associates (1985) *Sourcing '85* (New York: KSA).

Leonard-Barton, Dorothy (1987a) "A New CAE system for Shield Electronics Engineers", Harvard Business School Case Study.

Leonard-Barton, Dorothy (1987b) "Implementing new technology: the transfer from developers to operations", Harvard Business School, Division of Research, Working Paper 87–049.

Leontief, Wassily and Faye Duchin (1986) *The Future Impact of Automation on Workers*, New York: Oxford University Press.

Levy, Brian (1987) "Export Intermediation and the Structure of Industry in Korea and Taiwan", mimeo.

Levy, Brian, and Wen-Jeng Kuo (1987a) "The Strategic Orientations of

Bibliography

Firms and the Performance of Korea and Taiwan in Frontier Industries: Lessons from Comparative Case Studies of Keyboard and Personal Computer Assembly", mimeo.

Levy, Brian and Wen-Jeng Kuo (1987b) "Investment Requirements and the Participation of Korean and Taiwanese Firms in Technology-Intensive Industries", mimeo.

Mody, Ashoka (1986) "Recent Evolution of Microelectronics in Korea and Taiwan: An Institutional Approach to Comparative Advantage", Boston University Center for Asian Development Studies, Discussion Paper, No. 36.

Mody, Ashoka (1987) "Information Industries: The Changing Role of Newly Industrializing Countries", Paper presented to the Brookings Conference on Technology and Government Policy in Telecommunications and Computers, June 4–5, Washington, D.C.

Mody, Ashoka, and David Wheeler (1986) "Technological Evolution of the Semiconductor Industry", *Technological Forecasting and Social Change*, 30, pp. 197–205.

Mody, Ashoka and David Wheeler (1987a) "Towards a Vanishing Middle: Competition in the World Garment Industry," *World Development*, 15 (10/11), pp. 1269–1284.

Mody, Ashoka, and David Wheeler (1987b) "Prices, Costs, and Competition at the Technology Frontier: A Model for Semiconductor Memories", *Journal of Policy Modeling*, 9:2, pp. 367–382.

National Academy of Engineering (1982) *The Competitive Status of the U.S. Auto Industry* (Washington: NAE).

Nelson, Richard (1984) *High Technology Policies: A Five-Nation Comparison*, American Enterprise Institute for Public Policy Research, Washington.

OECD (1983) *Industrial Robots: Their Role in Manufacturing Industry*.

Ono, Keinosuke, and Odaka, Konosuke (1981) *Ancillary Firm Development in the Japanese Automobile Industry: Selected Case Stidues*, Working Paper, Institute of Economic Research, Hitotsubashi University, March.

Pelzman, Joseph (1982) "Economic costs of tariffs and quotas on textile and apparel products imported into the United States: a survey of the literature and implications for policies", *Weltwirtschaftliches Archiv*, Vol. 69, pp. 523–42.

Ramamurthi, Ravi (1985) *Brazil's Computer Strategy*, Harvard Business School Case Study, Boston.

Rhee, Yung Whee, Bruce Ross-Larson, and Garry Pursell (1984) *Korea's Competitive Edge: Managing the Entry into World Markets*, World Bank and John Hopkins University Press, Baltimore.

Roos, Daniel, *et al*, (1984) *The Future of the Automobile: The Report of MIT's International Automobile Program* (Cambridge, Mass.: MIT Press).

Rottenberg, Simon (1985) "The Allocation of Textile and Apparel Export Quotas Among Companies", CPD discussion Paper No. 1985–24, pp. 26–38.

Sahal, Devendra (1981) *Patterns of Technological Innovation*, Reading, Mass.: Addison-Wesley.

Salter, Malcolm *et al.* (1985) *"U.S. Competitiveness in Global Industries: Lessons from the Auto Industry"*, in Scott, Bruce, and Lodge, George (eds.) *U.S. Competitiveness in the World Economy*, (Boston: Harvard Business School Press).

Salter, Malcolm *et al.* (1986) *The Big Three: Struggling for Renewed Competitiveness*, Working Paper, Harvard Business School.

Scherer, Frederic M. (1978) "Technological Maturity and Waning Economic Growth", *Arts & Sciences*, 1 (Fall) pp. 7–10.

Scherer, Frederic M. (1984) "Using Linked Patent and R&D Data to Measure Interindustry Technology Flows", in Griliches (1984).

Smith, Donald (1985) "GM's Saturn Project: Workshop and Model of the Future", Paper presented at SITEV 85, Geneva, Switzerland, June 6.

Spence, A. Michael (1981) "The Learning Curve and Competition", *Bell Journal of Economics*, 12(1), pp. 49–70.

Sze, S.M. (1983) *VLSI Technology* (New York: McGraw-Hill).

Taylor, Alex (1987) "Who's Ahead in the World Auto War", *Fortune*, November 9, pp. 22–32.

Textile/Clothing Technology Corporation (1985) *News Release*, May.

Tigre, Paulo (1983) *Technology and Competition in the Brazilian Computer Industry*, New York: St. Martin's Press.

Toyobo Co., Ltd. (1985) "International Competition in the Textile Industry", mimeo, July 24.

Trajtenberg, Manuel (1985) "The Welfare Analysis of Product Innovations with an Application to CT Scanners", National Bureau of Economic Research Working Paper No. 1724.

UNCTAD (1986) *"Problems of Protectionism and Structural Adjustment"*, 1986, TD/B/1081 (Part 1), Table 8, p. 25.

Watanabe, Susumu (1984) *Microelectronics and Employment in the Japanese Automobile Industry*, Working Paper, ILO World Employment Programme Research (ILO: Geneva).

Wilson, Robert (1981) "Informational Economies of Scale", *Bell Journal of Economics and Management Science*, 6, pp. 184–95.

Womack, James (1986) "Prospects for the U.S.–Mexican Relationship in the Motor Vehicle Sector", Working Paper, Center for Technology, Policy, and Industrial Development, MIT.

Yoffie, David (1983) *Power and Protectionism: Strategies of the Newly Industrializing Countries*, New York: Columbia University Press.

Yuge, Yasushi (1987) "Automakers prepare to enter growing U.S. luxury market", *Japan Economic Journal*, September 26, pp. 1,19.

Index

Figures are in *Italic*; Tables are in **Bold**; (n) after a page number indicates note material.

DATE DUE

GAYLORD			PRINTED IN U.S.A.